PRAYER

A Handbook
for Today's Catholic

Reverend Eamon Tobin

LIGUORI
PUBLICATIONS

One Liguori Drive
Liguori, Missouri 63057-9999
(314) 464-2500

Imprimi Potest:
William A. Nugent, C.SS.R.
Provincial, St. Louis Province
The Redemptorists

Imprimatur:
Monsignor Maurice F. Byrne
Vice Chancellor, Archdiocese of St. Louis

ISBN 0-89243-300-0
Library of Congress Catalog Card Number: 88-83981

Scripture texts used are taken from the NEW AMERICAN BIBLE WITH THE REVISED NEW TESTAMENT copyright © 1986 by the Confraternity of Christian Doctrine, Washington, DC, and are used with permission. All rights reserved.

Part Two, Chapter 10, "Prayer of Reflective Spiritual Reading" was previously published in the *Review for Religious* in 1988. Part Two, Chapter 1, "Prayer of Thanksgiving" will appear in the *Review for Religious* during 1989. These chapters are used with permission of the editor of *Review for Religious*.

Excerpts taken from BEHOLD YOUR MOTHER, copyright © 1973 by the United States Catholic Conference, Washington, DC 20005, are used with permission. All rights reserved.

Excerpts taken from "Recovering the Rosary" (*America*, May 7, 1983) by Mitch Finley are reprinted with permission of America Press, Inc. All rights reserved.

Excerpts taken from PATHWAYS OF SPIRITUAL LIVING, copyright © 1988 by St. Bedes Publications, Petersham, MA, are used with permission. All rights reserved.

Excerpts taken from the English translation of THE ROMAN MISSAL, copyright © 1973, International Committee on English in the Liturgy, Inc., are used with permission. All rights reserved.

Excerpts taken from GOD AND YOU, copyright © 1988, Paulist Press, are used with permission. All rights reserved.

Excerpts taken from CHALLENGES IN PRAYER and SIMPLE PRAYER are from WAYS OF PRAYER, © 1982, Michael Glazier, Inc., and are used with permission. All rights reserved.

Excerpts taken from ABANDONMENT TO DIVINE PROVIDENCE by Jean-Pierre de Caussade, copyright © 1975; CENTERING PRAYER by Father Basil Pennington, copyright © 1982; and A CRY FOR MERCY by Father Henri Nouwen, copyright © 1983, are used with permission of Doubleday & Co., Inc. All rights reserved.

TABLE OF CONTENTS

DEDICATION

To the living and
the deceased members of my family,
the Tobins and the Brennans.

ACKNOWLEDGMENTS

The ideas expressed in this book are a combination of what I have discovered about prayer through my own efforts to pray and what I have learned from other praying pilgrims through their writing, tapes, seminars, and personal conversations. I am grateful both to those whom I quote directly in this book and also to those people whom I do not explicitly acknowledge because I either mislaid a book reference or because time has blurred what I have personally discovered from them.

I am especially grateful to the elder members of my family for being examples of people who constantly prayed. I saw them praying in the morning, in the midmorning, at noon, in the afternoon, in the evening, and late at night. My brothers and sisters and I could not help but get the message that prayer was a very important part of life.

I am grateful to Mrs. Maher, my elementary school teacher, and to the priests of St. Kieran's High School and Seminary whose dedication to prayer also sent me the right message about the vital importance of prayer in the life of a Christian.

I am grateful to all the people whose questions about prayer have kept me on a continuous search to understand a little more deeply the mysterious relationship that goes on between God and his people in and through prayer.

I am grateful to Sister Margaret Gilmore, S.N.D., who first encouraged me to write down my ideas on different aspects of Christian belief and practice and then to send them to a publisher.

I am grateful to all the people whose positive feedback to my earlier booklets has encouraged me to keep writing when I felt like quitting or when I thought I was too busy to write.

I am grateful to my friend and former pastor, Father Paul Henry, who in 1985 gave me the time to research this book despite the fact that we ministered in a very large and very busy parish. Also, thanks, Paul, for those "deep insights" received around the breakfast table.

I am grateful to Don and Chris Boland for their friendship and for the use of their home as a quiet place to write.

I am grateful to the men and women who read an earlier draft of this book: Jo Ann Perry, Mary Jo Nocero, Sisters Mary Kay Dunn and Karen Harper, P.C.P.A., Melannie Svoboda, S.N.D., Natalie DeLuca, M.H.S.H., and Fathers Nivard Kinshella, O.C.S.O., Tom Norris, Dan Bollard, Tim LaBo, and Tom Artz, C.SS.R. I thank each of you for your helpful suggestions regarding content and style.

I am grateful to the people at Liguori Publications whose acceptance of my first manuscripts helped me to recognize my gift for writing, and to Redemptorist Fathers Chris Farrell and Tom Artz who masterfully edited this book.

Finally, I am grateful to my good friend, Jo Ann Perry, without whose insights, encouragement, and expert assistance I would never have completed this book. Jo Ann offered countless suggestions and then patiently typed, retyped, and revised this manuscript more times than I can count. In addition, she has been a tremendous personal support and cheerleader in my efforts to spread the Good News through my writing.

PREFACE

Christ with me, Christ before me;
Christ behind me, Christ within me . . .
Christ in the heart of everyone
    who thinks of me;
Christ in every eye that sees me;
Christ in every ear that hears me.
                (Saint Patrick)

Remembering that I come from a race of people who for hundreds of years have been praying in the Christian way comforts, challenges, and sustains me in my efforts to be a praying person. Reflecting on the fact that my people have been a praying people for so many generations is a warm, comforting, and sustaining thought. It also challenges me to keep alive such a wonderful praying tradition and to add to it in some small way.

I am also comforted, challenged, and sustained by the fact that I come from a family for whom prayer was a very essential part of life. With affection I remember seeing my father kneeling on the kitchen floor while saying his "morning prayers" before going out to the fields to work all day. I remember my stepmother and my Aunt Daisy making their daily Holy Hour in the midmorning as they went about their morning chores. At midday everyone prayed the Angelus. It was especially edifying to see the big, strong men out in the fields stop their work, take off their caps, and silently pray, "The angel of the Lord declared unto Mary. . . ." After supper in the evening the whole family (and anyone else who happened to be there) got down on their knees and prayed the rosary. All of my aunts and uncles were people of prayer. Growing up in such an atmosphere reinforced in me, time and time again, the importance of prayer.

My grade school teacher was a very wonderful and prayerful lady. Consequently, prayer was an important part of my formation during my elementary school years. The high school which I attended as a boarder was run by diocesan priests. Daily Mass, morning and evening prayers, and visits to the Blessed Sacrament were integral parts of each day. Each year we also had a few two- or three-day retreats. My seven years in the seminary were in a very special way a time of formation in the varied ways of Christian prayer. Besides the spiritual exercises that were an essential part of daily life, each seminarian had a spiritual director with whom he could chat on a regular basis about his spiritual life.

Since my ordination to the priesthood in 1972, I have tried, with reasonable success, to remain faithful to an hour of *personal* prayer each day. In my parish work I have also had the opportunity to pray with diverse groups of Protestants and Catholics from whom I have learned much about the art of praying. I share these thoughts in order that you may know something of the background that I bring to this topic. In no way do I consider myself an expert in prayer. I am still very much a beginner and a learner. When it comes to prayer, all persons are perpetual students. Jesus alone is the Master, Teacher, and Expert.

Personally I find prayer (relating to God) to be both a consoling and difficult experience. It is consoling and enjoyable when I believe I am making contact with God whether on a feeling or faith level, when I discover new insights into his ways, when I receive answers to my petitions, and when I simply experience his loving presence and mercy. Praying is difficult for me when I am distracted or unfocused, when my prayer is dry, when I think my efforts to pray are going nowhere, and when I think I have lost contact with God.

I experience all of the common problems that people experience in prayer. I wonder how I should pray. I am often plagued by distractions in prayer. Sometimes I wonder if the time I spend in formal prayer could not be used more effectively. This question plus a busy schedule sometimes cause me to cut short my prayer time. I find it difficult to integrate prayer and life and see them as *one* act of worship before God. Sometimes I find prayer to be downright dull and boring, and I wonder how God could be interested or pleased by my feeble attempts to pray.

Despite all these difficulties I still find prayer to be absolutely essential to my life. Prayer is to my spirit what food is to my body. It is the bread of my spiritual life. To quit or neglect prayer is to quit or neglect to care for the core of my being (my spirit) and its deepest desire (intimacy with my Creator). Without prayer I would be a person without the wine of life (see John 2:3), a noisy gong and a clanging cymbal (see 1 Corinthians 13:1). Many, many years ago Saint Augustine said that all persons were created for communion with God and that their hearts would never rest until they rested in God. It is my strong belief in these words of Augustine that causes me to persevere in prayer and to say "no" (at least most of the time) to all of the things that compete with prayer for my time. I also try to remain faithful to prayer because as a minister of the Lord I deeply believe that without him I cannot be fruitful. In the Gospel of John, Jesus says:

> I am the vine, you are the branches.
> Whoever remains in me and I in him,
> will bear much fruit,
> because without me you can do nothing.
> (John 15:5)

Ministry not rooted in Jesus the Vine may have all the signs of success but in reality will be only "sound and fury signifying nothing" (Shakespeare). Ministry rooted in Christ *may seem* in the eyes of the world to be a failure, but in the eyes of Jesus it will be most fruitful. For those who are raised in a work-ethic, do-it-yourself society, it is not easy to come to believe that hours spent in quiet prayer can bring people closer to the kingdom than their own best laid plans and efforts. For me "wasting time" in prayer expresses my belief that it is God who is the Creator and Transformer of life, who makes the flowers grow and yields a rich harvest. When I begin to substitute work for prayer, I know I am believing the lie that proclaims, "If I work hard enough, things will really happen." This may be true in the secular realm, but it is certainly not true in the spiritual realm. In the latter, "things happen" when I generously cooperate with God's movement of grace at work in me and outside of me.

Despite the vast number of books available on prayer, I have decided to write another book because I believe each person, as a unique expression of God, can discover something unique about God and how to relate to him. Just as no two sunrises or smiles are exactly the same, no two persons approach prayer in exactly the same way. Therefore, when people speak or write about prayer — when they tell how they relate to God and how God works in them

— a new and unique image of prayer comes into being. Speaking more pragmatically, I decided to write this book on prayer because I wanted to gather together what I consider to be some keys to effective prayer (Part One) and some important traditional and contemporary forms of prayer (Part Two).

Even though the actual writing of this book took place over a period of two and a half years, it has, in another sense, been in the birthing process for about twelve years. Some twelve years ago I began a series of talks on prayer, and at each session I would give the participants a handout summarizing my main ideas. Each time I would give a new teaching on prayer, I would revise and update what I had previously written. The countless revisions reflected my own ongoing understanding of prayer, received from my own efforts to pray and from the suggestions of other people. By the time this manuscript is published, I will probably be ready to revise parts of it. This is so because the journey into prayer is an endless journey into the mystery of God. For this reason I constantly pray: "Lord, reveal your true nature to me and free me from my countless, distorted images of you and your ways."

In writing this book I have shared many of my beliefs and personal experiences of prayer. I ask your patience in bearing with me and my limitations. I especially ask you to keep in mind the fact that I am a product of my education, my upbringing, and my culture. Because of this and probably because I am a male, I regularly refer to God as "he." If your image of God is different, please do not toss aside this book just because I use male pronouns to refer to God. Rather, substitute your own words to describe God and continue to deepen your relationship with God.

Finally, this book is intended to be very practical. It is very much a how-to approach to prayer. For example, in Part One, I not only speak about some keys to effective prayer but I also offer practical suggestions on how to integrate such keys or basics into one's daily prayer life. In Part Two, I not only explain several different prayer forms but I also offer several examples of how to use them. Also, for personal or small-group use I offer, at the end of each key and each chapter, some *Reflection Questions* and a *Suggested Prayer Exercise*.

INTRODUCTION

He [Jesus] was praying in a certain place, and when he had
finished, one of his disciples said to him, "Lord, teach us to pray
just as John taught his disciples." He said to them, "When you
pray, say:
> Father, hallowed be your name,
>> your kingdom come.
>> Give us each day our daily bread
>> and forgive us our sins
>> for we ourselves forgive everyone in debt to us,
> and do not subject us to the final test."

(Luke 11:1-4)

People often ask: "What is prayer?" The answer to that question is not easy because there is no one definition of prayer that is
exhaustive. Most definitions have some element of truth to them,
but not one of them says it all. Because of this limitation, one
definition may be more accurate and helpful to some people while
another definition may be more accurate and helpful to others. It is
useful to share different ideas on the meaning of prayer because
such sharing can help us to clarify what it is we think we are doing
when we pray. It can also help us to become aware of definitions
that are not very accurate or helpful. We can only grow or go
forward if we are aware of where we are presently standing.

Here are two traditional definitions of prayer that are sometimes
criticized today. The first is this: "Prayer is the raising up of the
mind and heart to God." Some spiritual writers criticize this
definition because it seems to imply that the primary initiative in
prayer is ours and not God's, that *we* decide to pray. It would be
more accurate to say, "Prayer is our *response* to God's touch in our
lives." We pray or call out to God because *he has moved us* to pray
and not because we think it is a good idea to make contact with
God. The initiative is *always* with God. In him we live, move, and
have our being. We call out to God only because he has first called
out to us. We find God only because he has been looking for us (see

Genesis 3:8-9). A key truth to remember in the spiritual realm is that *all is gift*. We move toward God only because he is inviting us to come and enabling us to move in his direction (see Luke 10:21).

A second, frequently used definition of prayer describes it as "talking to God." Again the danger here is that we may think that in prayer the initiative is with us and not God. We need to keep in mind that if we talk to God it is only because he has moved us to talk to him. A second danger in using the "talking to God" theory of prayer is that we may think that prayer is basically a monologue wherein we do all the talking and God does all the listening. Central to growth in prayer is learning to listen to what God is saying and where he is guiding us.

Now here are some definitions of prayer that are more accurate than the previous two. Prayer can be defined as *opening to God*. In true prayer we expose ourselves to God as sunbathers expose themselves to the sun. Prayer is allowing God to love us and it is our becoming aware of God's great love for us. We become present and responsive to a God who is all around us and in whom we live, move, and have our being. Prayer is not an attempt to contact a missing, hard-to-find God. Rather it is our graced effort to be open, attentive, and responsive to a God whose presence fills the universe and who frequently becomes present to us in tangible ways. In the journey to Emmaus, we witness two disciples walking with Jesus (see Luke 24:13-35). At first they do not recognize him as Jesus. Only later did they really recognize who it was who had walked with them. In the same way, many of us may experience God, but we may not recognize the fact. Often only after a particular encounter or event do we recognize that God was present and active in our midst. Thus, a big part of prayer is learning to be sensitive to the "inbreakings" of God into the journey of life. To describe prayer as opening to God is particularly helpful when we find prayer difficult because the emphasis is not on *our* making things happen, but rather on our being *open* to what *God* might make happen.

Prayer can also be defined as the experience of *connecting* with God. There are some people we have known by sight for years, having seen them at church or at work, but we have never actually encountered them. Then one day we meet and talk. The potential for meeting or connecting was always there, but it has not happened until now. It is somewhat the same with God and prayer.

God is there — that is, within us and all around us — and we are there, but we just don't connect. A real "moment of prayer" happens when we are gifted with the grace of connecting with God.

Prayer can also be described as *waiting* upon the Lord. Day after day we go to prayer and wait. Sometimes we come away and we are still waiting, hoping, and expecting. But sometimes he comes and fills us with his light, giving us a tiny glimpse of who he is, and then he is gone. Then the waiting begins once again.

Prayer is *longing* for greater union with God. "As the hind longs for the running waters, so my soul longs for you, O God" (Psalm 42:2).

Prayer is *glimpsing* the beauty of God just as we get a glimmer of the sun now and again on a cloudy day.

Prayer is *standing before God* in radical poverty, without illusions, before the infinite richness of God.

Prayer is *discovering* all that God has already given us and growing in our appreciation of his gifts.

Finally, prayer can be defined as a personal relationship with God. Just as communication, properly used, is a tool that enables us to develop a close relationship with other human persons, so prayer is a tool that will make it more possible for us to develop a loving relationship with God. Consider the parallels. Generally speaking, our ability to relate to God will be no better than our ability to relate to other human beings. In fact, we can say that our style of relating on a human level will usually manifest itself in our prayer. For example:

- If we have a tendency to dominate human conversations, we will more than likely do most of the talking in prayer.
- If on the human level we usually wear our hearts on our sleeves, we will probably find it easy to reveal our true selves to the Lord.
- If we rarely give ourselves permission to express our tough feelings — anger, jealousy, inadequacy, and the like — we will probably not talk to God about such feelings. On the contrary, if we have become accustomed to "flying off the handle" with others, we will most likely not have a problem getting angry with God.
- If we find it hard to give and receive forgiveness on the human level, we may also find it hard to accept God's mercy and to

"forgive God" when he isn't moving in the way we think he should.

- If we are inclined to be utilitarian, manipulative, and controlling in our human relationships, we may consciously (but more likely unconsciously) bring the same attitudes into our relationship with God.

The way we are with people is the way we are with God. There is a danger that we fool ourselves into thinking that we are different with God than we are with people. Because we bring our style of communicating with others into our prayer, it is very important for us to be aware of our pluses and minuses in human communication.

Each of us is born with a potential to relate, a potential which must be developed if we are going to communicate effectively with other people. At this point in our lives, that potential to relate has been developed to a lesser or greater extent. If presently our human potential to relate isn't very good, that will diminish our potential to relate to God through prayer. For example, if we have very little ability to put aside our own concerns and preoccupations in order to be truly present to another, without a miracle of grace we are going to find it very difficult to hear the voice of God. Or if, on the human level, we have developed very little ability to trust others, we may find it hard to trust God. So each of us brings to prayer particular relational strengths and limitations which will probably either help or hinder our relationship with God.

Generally speaking, we can say that as we grow in our ability to relate on a human level we will be preparing good soil for our relationship with God. Married couples who participate in a Marriage Encounter weekend often report that their newfound ability to relate to each other also enhances their relationship with God. For example, just as the weekend helps them relate to each other more on a heart (sharing of feelings) than head (sharing of thoughts) level, so the weekend helps them relate to God on a heart or feeling level. It is through our human relationships that we develop the skills necessary to better our relationship with God.

While there are many parallels between human and divine-human communication, there are a couple of differences. An obvious one is that we cannot see God, hear his voice, or hold his hand. We have to depend on the gift of faith to believe that God is present to us and that he does indeed speak to us. A much more important difference is that in the divine-human relationship God is *always* faithful, loving, and merciful. God also has the power to bring about on a divine-human level something that seems unlikely or impossible on a human level. For example, even though we have never really trusted someone on a human level, it is possible that God could bypass our human limitation or heal it, thus enabling us to trust him. So while God usually works through our human gifts and talents, we must never limit God's work in our lives to such gifts and talents.

This Introduction has examined several definitions of prayer — none of which completely defines it because prayer remains a mystery. We have also seen that the meaning of prayer will change as our relationship with God develops. With this background we can now proceed to examine the four keys to an effective prayer life and explain the various types of prayer.

REFLECTION QUESTIONS

1. What insight in these pages made the greatest impression on you?
2. Which of the above attempts to define prayer appealed to you the most? How would you define prayer?
3. Can you see how we tend to bring our human way of relating into our prayer? Give some examples from your own life.
4. What was your experience with the prayer exercise suggested at the end of this chapter?
5. Did you disagree with or have trouble understanding any part of this section?

SUGGESTED PRAYER EXERCISE

Prayerfully read Psalm 139. Reflect on what this psalm tells us about prayer — about our relationship with God. What does the psalm tell us about God and about ourselves?

PART ONE

FOUR KEYS TO AN EFFECTIVE PRAYER LIFE

There are four essential keys to a genuine prayer life. Even though each of us prays in a different way, all of us should attend to these four basics in prayer: 1) We need to develop a positive image of God and self; 2) we must be honest with God; 3) we need to integrate prayer with daily life; 4) we must listen to God in prayer. If we are inattentive to any of these four keys, our relationship with God will be defective in some way.

Before examining each of these keys, it is important to understand the meaning of the words *key* and *effective* when used in connection with prayer.

Effective Prayer: On the human level our attempts to communicate with each other can be effective or ineffective. They may be ineffective because deep down (perhaps unconsciously) either one or both of the parties may not want to communicate. Sometimes the problem is that, despite the presence of good will, very little intimacy is experienced because of a lack of basic communication skills. Some people have poorly developed listening skills; others are unable to confront in a mature way and reconcile differences in a reasonable way. On the other hand, when two people want very much to communicate with each other and have developed some basic communication skills, there is every chance that they will experience a good degree of understanding, trust, acceptance, and intimacy.

Now just as there is effective and ineffective human communication, there is effective and ineffective divine-human communication. Some people, for example, pray (or rather "say prayers") all their lives and still do not make contact with God. Their prayer does not seem to affect their life or the way they communicate with other people. They are often harsh and critical of self and others, have little or no social conscience, and are fearful and anxious about the future. Obviously the prayer or communication of such people is ineffective and leaves much to be desired both with God and with others.

In contrast to such faulty communication, effective prayer, of its very nature, facilitates human and spiritual growth and enhances our relationships with others and with God. It leads to growth in faith, hope, and love of God, others, and self. Effective or real prayer helps us to face evil courageously and to place our trust in God when we walk in the valley of darkness (see Psalm 23). Effective prayer opens us to the experience of God's unconditional love and to the acceptance of his incomprehensible ways. It gradually helps us to be attentive and responsive to the needs of others, especially the poor. Finally, effective prayer should help us to accept and integrate the different dimensions and strivings of our being.

If these growth patterns are not developing in our lives, then maybe we should reevaluate our way of praying. Of course, the benefits of effective prayer will not happen overnight. In fact, there will be periods of time when we wonder if anything positive is happening in our prayer life. But over the long haul, we can expect to grow closer to God and to others if our prayer is honest and genuine.

Keys to Effective Prayer: The word *keys* does not imply that if we do certain things (press certain keys) we will *automatically* experience intimacy with God. Such belief would be seriously mistaken and blind to the fact that *in the spiritual life all is gift* and that union with God cannot be earned. The use of the word *keys* refers to some basic facts that we need to pay attention to so that we become *receptive soil* for God's transforming work in us. The phrase *receptive soil* reminds us that prayer and its goal, our transformation in Christ (see Galatians 4:19), are pure gift. All we can do is pray for this gift and do what we can to create the conditions that will make us good soil for God's transforming work. William Shannon, in *Seeking the Face of God,* writes: "It is true to say *we* don't pray, but rather *we let it happen in us.* The best we can do is to prepare and dispose ourselves to let it happen."

The following four sections will examine the four keys needed to help us prepare for an effective relationship with God.

KEY ONE:
DEVELOPING
A POSITIVE IMAGE
OF GOD AND SELF

God sent his only Son into the world so that we might have life through him. In this is love: not that we have loved God, but that he loved us and sent his Son as expiation for our sins.

(1 John 4:9-10)

If we really know ourselves to be loved by God, sooner or later our spontaneous response will be to love God in return. . . . The more rooted we are in love, the more generously shall we live our faith and put it into practice. . . . The knowledge that God loves us enables us to love ourselves without excuse and without questioning. We love ourselves as we are because our faith has convinced us that God does so.

(Peter G. van Breemen)

Few factors have the potential to affect the quality of our prayer life as much as our image of God and self. On a human level, the image and feelings we have for another person and how we perceive the other person to feel about us will usually have a tremendous effect on how we relate to that person. For example, we will approach and relate to a person whom we love and whom we perceive loves us in a different way than we will to a person for whom we have little or no feeling and whom we think does not particularly care for us. Also, our own self-image will affect the way we approach and relate to people. If we have a positive image of ourselves, we will go out to people and relate to them with confidence, assuming that they will like us. If we think we are not very lovable, we will approach people with self-doubt, fearful that they may reject us and not find us lovable. Also, if we believe that people will only accept us when we behave in certain ways, we will be inclined to be unreal with them, behaving only in ways that we perceive to be acceptable to them.

How is all this connected to our relationship with God and to our efforts at prayer? Well, God is a person and prayer is our attempt to relate with a personal God. We have already shown how the same basic dynamics are at work in our relationship with God as are at work in our relationships with other people. What helps or hinders us in our attempts to relate to other people will also help or hinder us in our relationship with God. Hence, when it comes to our relationship with God, some important questions to reflect on are these:

- How do we perceive and think about God? What images of God do we carry around inside us?
- Have we experienced God as loving us? Can we recall an example?
- Do we *like* God? Is God someone we really *like* to spend time with and talk to, someone whose company we enjoy? Or do we see God as a kind of *Divine Intruder* into our life, someone who has been pushed on us, someone we'd prefer not to have to deal with?
- Do we experience God as someone who cares about us very much, or do we perceive God as an aloof, distant Judge in the sky who is ready to pounce on us for our mistakes?
- Do we view God as a miserable miser or as someone who is generous and giving?
- Is relating to God basically an obligation that we must fulfill so that we are not locked out of heaven?
- Do we believe in a God who is demanding and who punishes us for our failings?
- Do we believe in a God who *actively* seeks us out when we have wandered far from the path to salvation (see Luke 15:4-7)?

It is very important that we spend some quality time reflecting on these questions and perhaps sharing our reflections with a spiritual guide. We need to check the images of God and self from which we operate and become aware of some of the consequences of these images. For example, if we perceive God to be a policeman-type person who imposes numerous rules and demands strict adherence to them, our relationship with him will be characterized by fear, by distance, and perhaps, by resentment. If we are overly scrupulous, we will believe consciously — or more likely unconsciously — that God is a tyrant who is impossible to please and who is ready to pounce on us for our failures. If we experience God as withholding himself from us, we will be reluctant to petition him for our needs. If we experience him as a loving Father, we will approach him with trust, relaxation, and love. If we experience God as merciful, we will not hesitate to talk to him about our failures, knowing that his love for us is not based on our good performance.

While we may at times *say* we believe in a God of love and mercy, our harsh, judgmental attitudes toward our own failures and those of others tell a different story. Sometimes there is quite a difference between the images of God that we *think* we have and the images of God that *actually* influence our lives. Most if not all of us carry around some primitive, destructive images of God which can particularly affect us in times of stress.

Once, while listening to a retreat leader speak about primitive images of God, I became aware that one of my primitive images is that God is a *demanding* person who is only pleased with me when I am being good and obeying his commandments. So while I may believe on an intellectual level in a God of unconditional love, I may function on an operational level with an image of God who loves me only when I am keeping the rules.

Our image of God often derives from childhood relationships with parents or authority figures. As I reflect on my relationship with my father, I become aware that I perceive him to be a good man but also a demanding man. Seemingly, I project the same demanding image onto God, and so I perceive God as difficult to please, loving me only when I am obeying the commandments.

The Scriptures give us several different and interesting images of God. God is described as the shepherd caring for his sheep (see Psalm 23); as the grocer providing food for the people (see Numbers 11:31); as a mother cherishing her offspring (see Isaiah 49:15) or weeping over her rebellious children (see Matthew 23:37-39); as teacher (see Matthew, Chapters 5–7); as healer of the sick and friend of sinners (see Luke 15); as one denouncing the righteous (see Matthew 23:13-32) and the corrupt (see Matthew 21:12-17); as challenger of the rich (see Matthew 19:16-26); and as one who demands all from a potential disciple (see Luke

9:23-26,57-62). Of course, no individual image or set of images can comprehend the Incomprehensible God. Saint Thomas Aquinas tells us: "If you can comprehend God, he is not God, for God is ultimately a Mystery." Nevertheless, it is legitimate for us humans, particularly at the early stages of our spiritual lives, to make use of human images to help us in our relationship with God.

IMAGING
GOD AS LOVE

Of all the images of God that can serve us well in our relationship with him, the image of God as unconditional lover is the most important. Insofar as we have not experienced God as love in the *deepest center* of our being (as opposed to acquired knowledge in the head), to that extent we have not experienced the Good News. It has been well said that the Good News is that God loves us, no strings attached; the sad news is that the vast majority of us do not believe the Good News with our heart.

God must sometimes get very frustrated with us as we ignore his efforts to convince us of his unconditional love. The primary reason he sent Jesus into the world was to reveal to us in a human way the extent of his love. When Jesus was dying on the Cross — with arms outstretched and blood pouring from his crucified body and heart — it was as if the Father was saying to every individual who was ever born: "This is how much I love you. My words are not empty; they are written with the blood of my own Son." The Scriptures tell us that Jesus died for us while we were still in our sins. Saint Paul writes:

Indeed, only with difficulty does one die for a just person, though perhaps for a good person one might even find courage to die. But God proves his love for us in that while we were still sinners Christ died for us.

(Romans 5:7-8)

When we doubt the truth of God's love, it is as if the power of original sin (expressed in a statement like "I wonder if I am really lovable") grabs hold of us. When such darkness invades our minds and hearts, we can reject it by renewing our baptismal vows in words like these: "Satan, I reject the lies you are now placing in my heart about my basic goodness. I believe that Jesus loves me with all my flaws and failures. Jesus, I believe this. Help me to dispel my unbelief.''

Of course, the main reason we doubt that God loves us unconditionally is that we may never have experienced unconditional love on a human level. Most of the time we experience love only when our behavior is acceptable to others: We try to be good so that others will love us. Consciously or unconsciously, we think it is the same with God. While we may *say* that God's love for us is not determined by our actions, our *behavior* often says that we actually believe that God loves us only when we keep his commandments. We try to be virtuous so that God will love us. In *The Christian Vision: The Truth That Sets Us Free,* Jesuit Father John Powell writes that God's response to this human thinking would be: ''O child of my heart, you've got it backwards. You shouldn't think that if you become more virtuous I will love you more, because already you have all my love as a free gift. You don't have to change so that I will love you more. What you really need to know is how much I have always loved you. Oh, then . . . you will really change.'' Sometimes we see the truth of these beautiful words when persons (perhaps alcoholics) fall in love and make dramatic changes in their lives. The experience of feeling loved by others motivates them to *want* to make changes in their lives and to *want* to respond with love. Love effects a change that no law and no amount of force could bring about.

In the Christian journey our primary aim is not to be good so that God will love us, but rather it is to be open to experiencing God's transforming love, which in turn will motivate us, more than anything else, to *want* to be Christlike in thought, word, and deed (see 2 Corinthians 5:14-21). This also reminds us to use some of our prayer time to be still before the loving presence of God so that he can communicate to us that we are loved by him regardless of our performance.

Unfortunately, most of us tend to be so busy or active in prayer that we fail to give God a chance to reveal his love to us. Yet this standing or sitting still before God is crucial for our spiritual growth. It is especially important to sit still before God when we are aware of specific sins that we have just committed. It is a healing grace for us to be able to face God with our sins and know that he still loves us. As we know, Jesus died for us *while we were still in our sin.* Christians are "loved sinners." Knowing this, not just in our heads but in our hearts, is indeed a tremendous grace.

Are there any practical suggestions that will help us to experience God's unconditional love? Yes, there are. Here are some worthwhile ones. *First,* we can pray for the gift of knowing in our hearts that God loves us. We can say: "Jesus, lead me more deeply into the unconditional love that our Father has for me." *Second,* we can try to recognize and name the particular ways that we believe God is presently loving us. Sometimes children don't recognize the many ways in which their parents are loving them. Likewise, we are often blind to the many ways that God is loving us. We need to work at becoming conscious of the simple ways in which God loves us in the flow of a day. A *third* suggestion is to try to develop a grateful attitude toward life, realizing that all the good and the apparently not good happenings in life come from the loving hand of God. *Fourth,* we should try to see an expression of God's love in the genuine expressions of love that people give us. The experience of intimacy with another readies our hearts to experience intimacy with God our Father.

Coming to prayer with a heartfelt (and not just head-wise) sense of God's compassionate love for us should help to make prayer much more relaxing. In the presence of a loving Father we don't have to prove anything, dress up nicely, or be formal. We are loved just as we are. Our loving Father says to us: "Come as you are; be yourself; enjoy your time with me. If you want to talk and pour out your heart about something, that's okay. If you want to rest in my presence, snuggle up in my lap and arms, that's okay, too."

IMAGING
OURSELVES AS LOVABLE

We need to remember that a key factor in an effective prayer life is experiencing ourselves as lovable. A poor self-image can play havoc with our relationships on both a human and spiritual level. When we suffer from a poor opinion of ourselves, we are inclined to assume that God (and other people) share this opinion. If we don't see much to love in ourselves, we will find it difficult to believe that God sees much to love in us. Such a belief will keep us at a distance from God. In effect, to question or deny our own goodness is like questioning or denying that we were created very good, as we are told in Genesis 1:31. Perhaps we should sometimes tell our Creator that we are sorry for the times we felt that he must have had an "off day" when he created us.

What can we do to come to a greater sense of our innate goodness and beauty? How can we begin to see ourselves as God sees us? The following are a few suggestions.

First suggestion: We can use the Word of God to transform and shape the way we see ourselves. Ultimately, our *self-image is formed by the loving Word of God or deformed by the destructive words of others.* Our self-image is shaped by the words we believe about ourselves. Which words are we listening to and believing, the affirming Word of God or the destructive words of others?

The only reason we end up with a poor self-image is because we allowed destructive words to enter and shape the core of our being. For example, some of us may believe we are stupid or no good. This happens because, at some point in our formation, someone said to us, "You are stupid and no good," and unfortunately we believed that person. The words, "I am stupid and no good," became part of how we saw ourselves. But — and this is a crucial point — the only reason why such words became a destructive force in our lives is because we dwelt on them, pondered them, and reflected on them so much that they reached not just our ears but the very core of our being where our self-concept is formed or deformed.

To counteract this, we must learn to dwell on, ponder, and reflect on the loving words of God and others. We do this when we allow the affirmation of God and others to touch not just our skin, as it were, but the very core of our being. But we allow the loving words of God and others to touch just our skin when we do not receive those words into our being and believe them. For example, we may receive an affirming letter from someone, quickly read it, toss it aside, and forget about the loving words written there. On the other hand, if we receive a negative letter, we may not only read it, but keep pondering it all day and perhaps for several days. How sad that so many of us tend to toss aside so easily the affirming words we receive while we tend to hold onto the negative, destructive words.

To help us as we listen to God's Word and allow it to affirm us in our self-worth, we will do well to consider the words of John's Gospel: "As the Father loves me, so I also love you" (John 15:9).

We begin by using our imagination to *visualize* Jesus speaking these words to us. We can imagine Jesus sitting on a chair across from us. He is looking at us with love and saying, "As my Father loves me, so do I love you."

Then we should try to allow those words to enter our being — to touch not just our ears but also our hearts. Perhaps we may wish to repeat the words of Jesus over and over again, giving them time to touch and shape the core of our being. We should recall everything that has been said about the importance of dwelling on the words spoken to us. Those words cannot bear fruit unless we reflect on them over and over again. Here we should imitate Mary who pondered the words that were spoken to her (see Luke 2:19).

Then we should verbalize our acceptance of the affirmation and love that Jesus offers. We can say, "Yes, Jesus, I believe you love me. Help me to believe it more deeply." So often we deny or fail to accept gracefully the affirmation offered to us by God and others. When the experience of affirmation and love is truly received and pondered, it has the power "to make us over again."

Then, having received, pondered, and accepted the word of affirmation, the next thing we need to do is thank God for his loving words. The act of giving thanks is a concrete sign that we have accepted God's word of affirmation. We could give thanks to God in simple words like this: "I thank you, Lord, for who I am. I thank you for making me precious in your eyes." Every time we feel negative about who we are or feel tempted to put ourselves down, we ought to affirm our God-given self-worth with that little prayer. Each of us has to learn to talk back to the negative voices inside and outside of us that threaten our self-worth. We can do this by constantly repeating: "Father, you have made me beautiful in your eyes. I praise you for the wonder of my being." (To learn more about this, see the Appendix of the book *The Healing Power of the Sacraments*, by Jim McManus, C.SS.R.)

Second suggestion: We can learn to believe more deeply in our own goodness if we see and receive Jesus in the Eucharist as a tangible sign of his tremendous love for us. At the Last Supper Jesus took bread and said, "This is my body, which will be given for you." Then he took the cup and said, "This cup is the new covenant in my blood, which will be shed for you'' (Luke 22:19,20). In and through these words Jesus is telling each of us: ''I am dying that you may live'' or ''I love you so much that I am ready to pour out my blood (my life) for you.'' Such words are truly awesome if only we could believe them deeply. Every time we receive Holy Communion, we are being offered an opportunity to affirm our belief in Jesus' love for us. Our ''Amen'' when we receive the Eucharist at Mass could very well mean ''Yes, Lord, I do believe you love me! Help my unbelief.''

Third suggestion: We can learn to accept ourselves as good and lovable if we risk sharing our true and false selves with other people. As we begin to reveal our dark or less noble side to another caring person and begin to experience his or her acceptance of us, this acceptance will help us to be more loving toward ourselves. Many people today are finding the therapeutic setting the best and the safest atmosphere in which to make true confessions. Good, caring therapists have both the training and the skills to communicate to their clients their unconditional acceptance. To decide not to reveal all of ourselves to another is to condemn ourselves to a life of loneliness and to be cheated of the opportunity to experience ourselves as unconditionally accepted and loved.

If we truly wish to transform the way we see ourselves, we have to be very patient. If for years we have believed negative and destructive lies about ourselves, we should not expect to change those beliefs overnight. Normally the transformation from a poor to a positive self-concept takes years, and even then we will sometimes find that we occasionally regress into believing negative things about ourselves.

We have treated the love of God and love of self separately in this section. In reality, of course, they are not separate; they are intertwined. As we grow in the experience of God's love, we will also come to see and experience ourselves as lovable.

REFLECTION QUESTIONS

1. What insight in these pages made the greatest impression on you?
2. Can you recall an experience when you felt loved and cherished by God?

3. What helps you to keep believing in God's love for you? What helps you to overcome doubts in this area?
4. What has helped you or helps you to believe in your own basic goodness? What circumstances can threaten or tear down your self-image?
5. Did you disagree with or have trouble understanding any part of this section?
6. After doing the suggested prayer exercise that follows, describe your experience.

SUGGESTED PRAYER EXERCISE

Take time to pray the Scripture texts listed below in the way suggested in this section. First, visualize Jesus speaking the words to you. Second, accept or receive the words of Jesus into your heart. Third, thank Jesus for his loving words.

"Because you are precious in my eyes . . . I love you" (Isaiah 43:4).

"Before I formed you in the womb I knew you, before you were born I dedicated you" (Jeremiah 1:5).

"As the Father loves me, so I also love you" (John 15:9).

KEY TWO:
BEING HONEST
WITH GOD

Moses again had recourse to the Lord and said, "Lord, why do you treat this people so badly? And why did you send me on such a mission? Ever since I went to Pharaoh to speak in your name, he has maltreated this people of yours, and you have done nothing to rescue them.

(Exodus 5:22-23)

How often we have mumbled the well-worn formula, "O my God, I am heartily sorry for having offended thee, and I detest all my sins because of thy just punishments. . . . " What I really want to say is: "I am not very sorry for my sins; in fact, I am rather fond of them, attached to them. I am not afraid of hell because I know you love me, but I would like to be different than I am." The point is we need to be honest before God with what is truly occurring in our life.

(Katherine Dyckman and Patrick Carroll)

In the initial stages of a human relationship, we usually make a special effort to be nice to the other person. We tend to avoid talking about issues or feelings that may cause embarrassment or a rift in the relationship. Also, if we are trying to make an impression on the other person, we may make a special effort to come off "looking good." We may use masks to cover up the areas of our personality that we do not like or think the other party wouldn't like. In other words, our tendency will be to edit what we show or reveal to the other. Yet to the extent that we are failing to share our true thoughts and feelings, the relationship is lacking in honesty and genuineness.

For example, we may be angry with a friend but choose not to reveal our feelings of anger. We act as if "everything is just fine," when, in fact, we might be quite angry inside. Such conduct usually has a detrimental effect on the relationship — making it become merely polite, bland, and boring. We begin to talk about external things — like the weather and other people — rather than sharing personal feelings. An atmosphere of "cool distance" replaces intimacy. Often the repressed anger will reveal itself in passive-aggressive behavior. Until the anger is dealt with, the relationship will remain polite and at a cool distance. When the anger is admitted, talked about, and dealt with, the relationship begins to progress and closeness is restored.

For most of us, telling other persons that we are angry with them is far from easy. Very few of us feel comfortable in expressing our anger. Hence, our tendency is to repress our anger and pretend it doesn't exist. Thus the decision to confront difficult feelings or issues in a relationship is a *decision to love*. We make a decision to reach out because we care about the relationship and because we trust in the goodness of the other to understand whatever it is we need to share. In friendships we learn over and over that we enjoy each other's company to the extent that we decide to be honest and genuine with each other.

So it is in our relationship with God. If we are honest and open with God, we will feel close to the Lord most of the time. On the other hand, if we treat God as "polite company," we may find that while we have a "nice" relationship with God, it lacks fire and intimacy. We will probably experience God as a distant figure.

Learning to be open and honest with God is, without a doubt, one of the most difficult lessons that we have to learn in the school of prayer, especially if our tendency in human relationships has been to hide our real thoughts and feelings. It is not easy to tell others, not to mention the Other — God, the perfect One — that we are angry with them or jealous of them or that we don't feel like communicating with them. And yet if the relationship is to grow and mature, that is exactly what we must learn to do.

ADMITTING
OUR FEELINGS

Many of us have been taught that being angry at God is a sin. As a consequence we are consciously or unconsciously afraid to tell God that we are angry with him. We may think that if we get angry with God he will strike back and punish us. (Perhaps that was our experience as a child when we got angry with our parents, so we learned to hide and not express our anger.) Spiritual directors tell us that most of us are unconscious of our anger with God. For example, if we think that life is unfair, we may unconsciously blame God and be angry with him for allowing such injustice. In his book, *God and You,* Jesuit Father William Barry writes:

> We might resent being the second-born in the family where it seems the oldest gets all the attention and where we always seem to be second best. We may resent the loss of a parent in childhood through death or divorce. We may have grown up as a member of a harassed minority. We may have a physical deformity or blemishes that have made us the objects of stigmatization by others. *Even if our heads tell us that God is not to blame for these lacks, still they are life's hurts, and the anger and resentment we feel may also be aimed at the Author of life.* At the least, we may at some level feel that God, the all-powerful, could have spared us or protected us if he really loved us.

In the same chapter of that book, Father Barry goes on to tell the story of a young woman who had experienced a personal relationship with God. However, since her engagement to be married, she found God to be distant and prayer to be boring. Initially, she did not know the cause of her alienation. It was only gradually and with the help of a spiritual director that she realized that she was very angry that her father, who died when she was five years old, would not be present at her wedding to walk her down the aisle. It was only later still that she realized that she was angry with God that he had taken her father. One day she went to church to thank God for the blessings in her life. But when she tried to pray, images of her wedding flooded her mind. She became enraged that her dad would not be present. She imagined herself going down the aisle alone, showing everyone the terrible thing God had done to her when he took her father. Then she proceeded to express her anger with God in no uncertain terms. Reflecting on her experience, the young lady realized that God had listened to her expression of anger with patience and compassion. The wall between her and God was broken down. God was experienced as closer, and prayer was no longer boring.

31

An important appendix to the story is that the young lady was not completely freed of her anger during that one prayer experience in church. Periodically, during the weeks following, her anger would flare up anew. Each time this happened she expressed her anger and found that God listened to her patiently and with compassion.

This touching story teaches us several lessons. It teaches us that it is possible to be angry with God about what happened to us years ago. It reminds us about our tendency to repress our anger with God. It shows us that expressing anger at God doesn't drive him away. Instead, it brings him closer to us. Finally, the story teaches us that if we are angry with God about something, we may have to express that anger not just one time but several times.

The prophet Jeremiah can teach us how to be up front with God. Jeremiah was a rather quiet and gentle person, but his "soul-conversations" reveal that sometimes he engaged in some tough dialogues with God. We are very fortunate that his book in the Hebrew Scriptures contains many of his "confessions" or soul-conversations. Being a gentle person, Jeremiah was particularly sensitive to outbursts of hostility from the people he was trying to reach. Once when experiencing such hostility, he cried out in desperation:

> Cursed be the day
> on which I was born!
> May the day my mother gave me birth never be blessed!
> Cursed be the man who brought the news
> to my father, saying,
> "A child, a son, has been born to you!"
> filling him with great joy.
>
> (Jeremiah 20:14-15)

In another chapter, Jeremiah complains to God about the injustice of allowing evil people to prosper. He even has some suggestions for God concerning how he ought to deal with the wicked (see Jeremiah 12:1-3).

Jeremiah also questions God about how he treats his servant and wonders if God has been lying to him (see Jeremiah 15:10-21).

For most of us, speaking to God like Jeremiah did is unthinkable. Yet the Scriptures provide many examples of such honest, heartfelt questioning of God and his ways. The Psalms in particular contain many such soul-conversations (see Psalms 22 and 38). The following passages give examples of how open and honest Moses was in his relationship with God: Exodus 5:22-23, Exodus 32:11-14,30-32, Exodus 33:12-23, Numbers 11:10-15, and Numbers 14:13-19.

We all recognize the fact that even friends become frustrated and angry with each other once in awhile. They get upset when their plans are ignored or when they think their friends are inattentive to their needs and are ignoring them. We must wonder about a relationship where no anger and frustration are experienced. Many spiritual guides tell us that if we are "stuck" in our prayer life, we will often begin to move again when we are able to recognize and express our anger toward God, people, and life.

Several years ago I attended a seminar given by the late Jesuit priest from India, Father Anthony de Mello. In the course of the weekend he told of how he would never forget the night he went to bed telling Jesus he didn't *like him* because he felt he (Jesus) had been pushed on him. He said it was far from easy to express such feelings to Jesus. But the next morning when he got up, he felt better and closer to Jesus. Their relationship was now more real.

In dealing with the whole area of being angry with God, it might be good to keep in mind that some spiritual guides believe that certain personalities — more so than others — may be less inclined to feel angry with God. (See Barbara Metz, S.N.D. de N., and John Burchill, O.P., *The Enneagram and Prayer*.)

It is not only unexpressed anger at God that will cause distance between God and us. We will also create a wall between God and ourselves if we fail to honestly recognize and deal with other feelings that we have toward other people. For example, we may experience feelings of hate, jealousy, fear, lust, guilt, or similar attitudes. As long as such feelings are not dealt with, it is most likely that we will experience a barrier between God and us.

DEALING
WITH OUR FEELINGS

Many of us were raised to believe that certain feelings like anger, hate, jealousy, and lust were wrong and sinful. But the good news is that feelings are neither right nor wrong. Rather, feelings, like the clouds (bright or dark), simply exist. There is no such thing as an immoral feeling. *All* feelings, even hate, fear, and jealousy, are good in themselves and have a role to play in our lives. For example, our capacity to feel hate is helpful in the face of sin and evil. We use the feeling of fear to stop us from stepping off a ten-story building. We can have a love that is jealous (in the protective and not possessive sense) for the welfare of our children and loved ones. The question of morality arises only when we express our feelings in inappropriate ways or when we allow our feelings to control our behavior. For example, it is not wrong to have hateful feelings for others. Nor is it wrong to tell them in a kind way that we have feelings of hatred toward them. But it would be wrong for us to allow our feelings of hate to cause us to behave in hateful ways toward others. This can be particularly cruel and confusing when we haven't even told the other person that we are very upset with him or her.

An important part of human and spiritual growth is learning to accept and integrate all of our feelings. We need to be aware of what feelings are unacceptable to us and why. Our so-called negative feelings often flow from some unresolved past hurt or from an upbringing that communicated to us that certain feelings were wrong and bad. If all our lives we have believed that certain feelings (like jealousy, hate, lust, anger, and similar emotions) are wrong or at least unacceptable, it will not be easy for us to move to a point where we easily accept *all* feelings as okay in themselves. It will take time, patience, gentleness, and usually the support of others — including a caring counselor — to help us embrace and treat like a wounded child those feelings in us that we were trained to believe were unacceptable and sinful. This is not a blank check to allow our feelings to control us and run our lives. Rather, it is an exhortation to stop pounding on ourselves for having certain feelings or fantasies. We need to learn how to deal with our feelings as we would deal with a wounded or unruly child — namely, with a combination of gentleness and firmness.

I often use a spiritual journal to help me deal with my tough or uncomfortable feelings. Here are four methods that I use.

First, name the feeling. By simply *naming* an intense feeling that is controlling us, we immediately rob it of some of its power.

Second, express the feelings. If our intense, "negative" feelings are toward a particular person, we should imagine that person sitting opposite us and telling him or her exactly how we feel. We hold nothing back. Actually, the very act of forcefully expressing our true feelings defuses their intensity. It cannot be emphasized enough how important it is to *give expression* to our feelings *before* we pray for their healing.

Third, own the feelings and accept them as part of who we are. It is not easy for any of us to admit that sometimes we have feelings of jealousy, inadequacy, hate, and so forth. Each of us probably has our own list of feelings that we particularly find very difficult to accept. Much of the shadowy, unconscious side of our personalities consists of feelings that we judge to be unacceptable. The result is that we push such feelings into our unconscious and refuse to relate to them. Unfortunately, such feelings, like an unruly child, continue to exert a negative influence in our lives and will continue to do so until we enter into a reconciling relationship with them.

One way for us to grow in our acceptance and ownership of our unacceptable feelings is by dialoguing with them as we would dialogue with an unruly child or a friend with whom we have had a disagreement. We can use our imagination to personify the internal feeling with which we want to dialogue. We can give the feeling a name (call him "Red Anger" or her "Jealous Susie") and imagine him or her sitting down opposite us. We might begin the dialogue in this fashion:

You/Self: I hate admitting that you are a part of my household. I just hate the control that you sometimes have over me. I also hate the way you make me feel inside.

Red Anger: I know how much you dislike me and wish I didn't exist. Nevertheless, I am glad that you have finally decided to take a few minutes to talk to me. For so long you have ignored me and pushed me away into some dark corner of your heart.

You/Self: You're right. I have ignored you and a part of me even now wants to continue to ignore you. Frankly, I just hate to think that you are a part of me, and that is why I usually push you away when you show yourself. Yet I know for my own peace and integration that I must recognize your presence, learn to talk to you, and even befriend you.

Red Anger: Good. I'm delighted that you want to talk to me. I know that I can cause you much grief — especially in that part of you that likes always to be in control. Perhaps my presence and intensity wouldn't be so bad if you learned not to panic when I appear on the scene. Instead, just be there for me — listen to me as you would listen to a friend who is very angry or to a child who is upset about something.

You/Self: You know, Red Anger, I feel better already. Just the act of recognizing your presence and talking to you defuses a lot of heat and replaces it with feelings of peace and quiet. Perhaps you are not the horrible creature I thought you were, and if I would give you a little more recognition and attention, you would not create such havoc inside of me.

This conversation is a concrete example of how we can begin to bring peace and reconciliation to feelings and parts of us that we would rather ignore. We all know that we feel better when we choose to talk to an enemy in our external lives. Why should it be any different with our internal enemies? Each of us has a number of them (skeletons in the closet) whose existence we have never admitted, let alone dialogued with. Jesus commands us to love our enemies (see Luke 6:27-36). But what if our biggest enemies live within? Growth and integration as human and spiritual persons involve learning to relate to our inner voices, feelings, and figures — learning to befriend the enemy within. Whenever we take the time to engage in such dialogue, we invariably feel more peaceful and integrated. We feel like we do after we have decided to talk to a friend with whom we have had a falling out. (Three good books to read about dialoguing and healing our feelings are: Morton Kelsey's *The Adventure Inward* and *The Other Side of Silence* and Eddie Ensley's *Prayer Feeling and Healing Our Emotions.*)

Fourth, talk to Jesus about these feelings and seek his healing. It is important and consoling to remember that Jesus, being fully human, probably experienced at times all the feelings with which we feel uncomfortable. In fact, it is very helpful if we can find and reflect on an incident in Scripture where Jesus had a feeling similar to ours. For example, if we feel angry we can meditate on the Temple scene where Jesus became angry with the buyers and sellers (see John 2:13-22). In praying to the Lord about our feelings, we might ask him to help us see why a particular encounter or event sparked off certain feelings in us. Perhaps we feel jealous of someone else's gifts because we are unaware or unappreciative of our own gifts. Perhaps we got very angry with someone because he or she told us a truth we didn't want to hear. When we find within ourselves uncaring feelings for another person, we need to ask Jesus to give us a new heart toward that person (see Psalm 51).

Of course, learning to be honest with God involves more than dealing with uncomfortable feelings. Dealing with our feelings, especially the feeling of anger, has been made the main focus of this section because it is an area in which most of us have received very little spiritual guidance, and often the guidance we received was, unfortunately, more destructive than helpful to our human and spiritual growth.

In summary, we need to realize that learning to be real and honest with God involves bringing our whole selves before God: our messy selves, our confused selves, our good selves. It involves learning to talk to God about our relationships, our jobs, our possessions, our sexiest, wildest, most cruel thoughts, feelings, fantasies, and desires. It involves talking to God about our money: how we make it and how we spend it. It involves talking to God about how we use our time and talents. If we really want to know what is important to us, all we need to do is check and see how we use our time, treasure, and talents.

Honesty in prayer will involve bringing before the Lord our doubts, fears and the anger we may have toward God, others, and self. It may involve telling God that we are sorry for some sins but not so sorry for others, at least at this time. It may involve telling God that we are not yet ready to surrender to him certain areas of our lives. Such openness and honesty about our real self will not happen overnight. It will take time and usually the support and encouragement of a soul-friend. In fact, we are only truly genuine with ourselves, others, and God on rare occasions. But we should treasure such moments because they are moments of true encounter. Honesty with God, others, and self demands a huge amount of courage and humility. We ought to pray frequently for such courage and humility.

REFLECTION QUESTIONS

1. What insight in these pages made the greatest impression on you?
2. Do you tend to treat God as "polite company," or do you tend to level with God about the important matters in your life?
3. Why do you think people would hesitate to talk to God about certain parts of their lives? Why might you hesitate?
4. Have you ever risked an honest "moment" with God like the example given by Father de Mello in this section? If so, what happened? How did it feel?
5. Did you disagree with or have trouble understanding any part of this section?
6. After doing the suggested prayer exercise that follows, describe your experience.

SUGGESTED PRAYER EXERCISE

Choose an area or feeling in your life about which you have never talked to God. Write a letter to the Lord about this forgotten or "forbidden" area or feeling. Then try to jot down what you think God's response to you might be. Later, have a dialogue with one of your troublesome feelings in a way similar to what was demonstrated on pages 35-36.

KEY THREE:
INTEGRATING PRAYER
WITH DAILY LIFE

The apostles gathered together with Jesus and reported all they had done and taught. He said to them, "Come away by yourselves to a deserted place and rest a while."

(Mark 6:30-31)

Unless the prayers we speak are tightly linked with the lives we lead, they will be babblings we hide behind rather than true speech which reveals who we are in relation to all that is.

(John Shea)

One of the biggest challenges of the spiritual journey is the integration of prayer (our relationship with God) to the rest of life. Most of us, particularly men, have a tendency to compartmentalize life. We give sections of our day to work, family, and recreation, and only then do we allot to God a portion (too often a leftover portion) of our day. There is, of course, a real sense in which we need to compartmentalize the activities of our day if we are to properly concentrate on each activity. From a spiritual point of view, however, such compartmentalization would be very destructive if it meant the exclusion of the Lord from the secular activities of our day. If Jesus is to become *Lord* of our life, he must be invited to guide and permeate *every* activity of our day. When this happens our whole day — with its religious and secular dimensions — will become one act of worship to the Father. Jesuit Father Richard Hauser, in his book entitled *In His Spirit: A Guide to Today's Spirituality,* writes: "The holiest actions of our day are those done most in tune with the Spirit: These may be either prayer or service."

Authentic spirituality does not separate formal prayer and secular activities because the same Spirit is present and active in all of them. Ideally one complements the other. True prayer imbues our action with the Spirit of Christ, and action done in God's Spirit not only sanctifies us but also prepares us for formal prayer.

The spiritual life is all of life: cooking, paying bills, driving to work and little league games, making love, and dealing with conflicts. God isn't just present in the "holy things" like the Eucharist, the Church, and the Bible. God is present in all encounters, events, and objects. Moses met God in a burning bush. Every bush or event in life is burning with the presence of God, if only we have the faith to see it. The challenge is not just to do a few spiritual exercises every week when we attend Mass, read the Bible, or pray the rosary. The challenge is to make every encounter and event of our week a spiritual exercise through which we grow in our relationship with God. The more we do this the more real God will become for us. God will become a companion with whom we share all of life — not like a doctor whom we call when we need some help or like a boss with whom we exchange daily greetings and niceties but with whom there is no personal relationship. The more we compartmentalize God and box him in, the more unreal he will be to us and the more we will be alienated from him. Perhaps one reason why God allows our prayer life to dry up is because we have stopped looking for the Lord in the laundry room, the store, or the office.

INTEGRATION
THROUGH OCCUPATIONAL
AND SPOUSAL PRAYER

How do we go about integrating prayer with our daily life? One way is to make careful use of what William McNamara, O.C.D., in his book, *The Human Adventure,* calls occupational and spousal prayer. Occupational prayer takes place while we are on the job of daily living. Spousal prayer happens when we rest from all activity so that we can be totally present and available to God, our Divine Spouse. (Notice that spousal prayer describes our relationship to God as our spouse and does not refer to one's marital status or state in life.) Both forms of prayer — occupational and spousal — are important and interdependent. One feeds into and needs the other.

Occupational prayer is the daily dialogue we have with God as we go about the daily tasks of life and behold the beauty of creation. We accept the fact that the spiritual life encompasses all of life. Occupational prayer makes that statement a reality in our lives. It is the kind of prayer that can give quality and power to the mundane, pedestrian affairs of life. When we pray as we go about the work of our day, God will be our partner in cooking meals, changing diapers, conducting business affairs, playing tennis, making hospital calls, driving the car — whatever we do on the occupational level.

Susan Muto, in *Pathways in Spiritual Living,* describes her occupational prayer in this way:

> Morning dawns. I awaken slowly and take an extra moment to say thanks to God for the gift of this day. While dressing, I try to center my thoughts on the Lord: "Even if I do not think of you explicitly, let me do what I do for your sake." I eat and feel grateful for the food on my table. While driving, I can still take a few moments for recollection. I stop at the traffic light and look over the hills, knowing that his presence is everywhere. I intersperse mental plans for my morning with brief meditations on his providential care. . . . By the time I arrive at the office, my working day has already taken on a deeper meaning. What might have been a merely functional approach is replaced by a rhythmic blend of action and contemplation, labor and leisure and all because of a shift in attitude . . . .

For occupational prayer to have depth it will need to be backed up with regular periods of spousal prayer. Sometimes the popular slogan, "My work is my prayer," is used as an excuse for not setting aside time for spousal prayer. This is indeed an unfortunate error in spiritual living that keeps our relationship with the Lord superficial. Spiritual directors all agree that only by seeking to be exclusively present to the Lord through spousal prayer on a regular basis will we grow in our ability to be present to God all of the time through occupational prayer. The document *Spiritual Renewal of the American Priesthood* (published by the United States Catholic Conference) reminds us that when everything is prayer, nothing is prayer and without prayer we perish. When we attempt to find God everywhere but in no particular place, we tend to find him nowhere. Those who pray on the job also need to enter their room and pray to their Father in secret.

The quality of our presence to the encounters and activities of daily life will be in direct proportion to the quality of our presence to God who is the Ground of all presence.

The importance of regular periods of exclusive time with the Lord (that is, spousal prayer) cannot be stressed too much. Unfortunately, most people seem to lack conviction about the pressing need for regular periods of spousal prayer. Yet if Jesus and all the saints through the ages found the need for regular periods of spousal prayer, surely we lesser mortals should be able to see our need for such times of prayer.

I often remind people that there are 1,440 minutes in every day and 96 fifteen-minute periods. Then I ask: "Can you truthfully say you are serious about your relationship with God if you do not give one or two of the 96 fifteen-minute periods in every day to God or twenty or thirty of the 1,440 minutes?" Then I continue: "If at this time in your spiritual journey, giving the Lord fifteen or thirty minutes a day is not part of your daily schedule, I suggest that you reflect on why it isn't."

PRETEXTS
FOR NOT INTEGRATING

Some people are fearful of integrating their prayer life with their daily life. Here are some of the excuses they use:

- "I'm too busy." This certainly is true for most of us. We feel overscheduled to death. Yet the deeper issue is the lack of conviction about the vital importance of spousal prayer for our spiritual health and growth. Isn't it remarkable how people with kidney problems and with very busy schedules make time for two-hour visits to the hospital three times a week for dialysis? None of these people would ever dream of saying to the doctor, "Sorry, doctor, I can't do it; I'm too busy." We always have time for what is important to us.
- "Formal or spousal prayer is just for priests and religious and very dedicated lay people, but not for the ordinary Catholic." The truth is that *all* of God's children are called to a life of

holiness. The bishops assembled for the Second Vatican Council in the early 1960s stressed that the call to holiness is universal.

> The Lord Jesus . . . preached holiness of life to each and every one of his disciples regardless of their situation. . . . All the faithful of Christ of whatever rank or status are called to the fullness of Christian life and to the perfection of charity (*Dogmatic Constitution on the Church*, #40).

- "I'd have no idea of how to spend twenty minutes of quiet time with the Lord." This is actually true for most lay people — hence, the importance of books like this.
- "I used to have a daily quiet time, but I quit because I felt I was making no progress, going nowhere." This reveals the problem of dryness which will be dealt with in Chapters Thirteen and Fourteen.
- "I don't want to get too serious about prayer because — consciously or unconsciously — I'm afraid of losing control over my life." At the heart of authentic prayer is surrender to the will of God. Because we fear this surrender and where it leads — to the Cross — most of us keep God at arm's length. We may frequently "say prayers" or read Scripture often, but we may not listen properly because we are afraid of what God might say to us or ask of us.
- "I don't want to listen too closely to God in prayer because I'm afraid of what the Lord might say to me." He might ask something of us that we are not ready to give, or he may reveal to us something about ourselves that we would prefer not to hear. All the spiritual masters tell us that growth in self-knowledge is an essential ingredient of human and spiritual growth. We all create a certain ideal image of ourselves which we try very hard to protect. We are not very open to allowing God an opportunity to crack that ideal self-image by revealing to us a less perfect side. Also, most of us are afraid of being found by God. Like Adam and Eve, we often hide when we think God is coming our way (see Genesis 3:8).

Building into our schedules a regular quiet time with the Lord is, without doubt, one of the most important actions we can perform to facilitate our spiritual growth. It is not, however, an easy discipline to develop. Most people who give the Lord a special quiet time on a regular basis will witness to the fact that it took much cooperation with God's grace to develop the discipline of spousal prayer. Most of us need the encouragement and the reinforcement of a spiritual director or a small group of soul-friends to begin and maintain a conviction about the value of regular times of spousal prayer with God.

If spousal prayer is presently not a part of our prayer life, we can begin now to ask God to place in our hearts a desire to spend a daily quiet time with him. Then, as we feel led, we can begin to spend fifteen to twenty minutes of daily quiet time with him. Part Two of this book will offer some suggestions on how to spend a quiet time with the Lord. (One of the best tools to help us integrate prayer and life is the Consciousness Examen explained in Chapter Seven.)

REFLECTION QUESTIONS

1. What insight in these pages made the greatest impression on you?
2. Does your relationship with God presently include regular times of *spousal* prayer? If not, why not? If so, how did you come to a conviction about the importance of spousal prayer and how do you usually spend that time?
3. What problems do you face as you try to integrate prayer or gospel values with the rest of your life? What helps and hinders you in this challenge?
4. Did you disagree with or have trouble understanding any part of this section?
5. After doing the suggested prayer exercise that follows, describe your experience.

SUGGESTED PRAYER EXERCISE

Take Jesus on a tour of your life. Invite him to enter every area: work, relationships, finances, sexuality, recreation, prayer, whatever. Try to speak to him honestly about each one of these. Notice the times when you feel happy and comfortable with him and notice the times when you feel awkward, hesitant, and uncomfortable. Be in touch with the feelings you experience as you move from one area to another.

KEY FOUR:
LISTENING TO GOD
IN PRAYER

Oh, that today you would hear his voice:
  Harden not your hearts. . . .

(Psalm 95:7-8)

To listen is much more difficult than to speak. When we speak
we are the center of attention. We enjoy this. However when we
listen the other becomes the center of attention and that is much
more demanding. To listen means that . . . we must empty ourselves in order to be filled with the other person.

[In prayer] listening implies being open to what God wants to do
in us and also being ready to respond to God.

(David E. Rosage)

In the verse of Scripture quoted above, God is pleading with
Israel to listen to his voice and direction. Because they often
refused to listen to God, the Israelite people brought much hardship on themselves and were not as close to God as they could have
been. They spent many years journeying a few miles in the desert.
The journey would have taken them a much shorter time if they had
learned to hear and obey God's leading and direction.

One of the main reasons why many of us make slow progress in
the spiritual life is because we never develop an inner spiritual ear
with which to listen to the leadings of God's Holy Spirit. In his
book, *Opening to God,* Jesuit Father Thomas Green writes, ''Listening is a real art which some people never learn. We all have
experienced people who cannot or do not listen. They hear but they
do not understand; their bodily ears pick up sound, but their hearts
are not attentive to its meaning. . . . The good pray-er is above all a
good listener.''

We should not try to dominate the time we spend with God. In the Scriptures we read where the young boy Samuel says to God, "Speak, Lord, for your servant is listening" (1 Samuel 3:10). It seems many of us have misread that text, thinking that it says, "Listen, Lord, your servant is speaking." So often in prayer we speak too much and listen too little. In theory we may believe that what God has to say to us is much more important than what we have to say to God, but in practice we act as if what we have to say is the more important of the two. We rush into our place of prayer, say our prayers, do our reading, and then rush away without ever giving God any chance to speak to us. If we treated our friends like this, we would lose them. God created us with two ears and one mouth, hoping perhaps that we would listen twice as much as we would speak. If that was God's intention, not very many of us got the message.

NECESSARY
ATTITUDES FOR LISTENING

True listening in prayer is a real challenge, demanding faith, selflessness, patience, a reflective attitude, and courage.

We need *faith* to believe that God does communicate with us, his people; and we especially need faith to believe that God really does want to speak to us personally.

We need *selflessness* because listening always demands the ability and willingness to put aside our own need to talk or our desire to be center stage, so that we can listen to others and give them center stage.

We need *patience* because God does not always speak to us according to our time schedule. He tells us so himself, "Nor are your ways my ways" (Isaiah 55:8).

We need to develop a *reflective attitude* toward life so that we can learn to read God's messages as they come to us in the events and encounters of daily life.

And, of course, true listening demands *courage* because God sometimes asks us to travel places we'd prefer not to go. Remember the story of Jonah who took the first ship out of port to get away from God (see Jonah 1:1–2:11). Recall what Jesus himself said to Peter at the end: "When you grow old . . . someone else will dress you and lead you where you do not want to go" (John 21:18).

We should pray often for a *desire* to hear God's voice and for the above mentioned dispositions that enable us to hear and respond to the Word of God. In the spiritual life *all is gift*. Hence, we must constantly pray for the dispositions of heart that will facilitate our growth in Christ.

In his book, *Opening to God,* Father Green titles Chapter Two, "The Irrelevance of Prayer," and Chapter Three, "The Relevance of Prayer." When I first read the title of Chapter Two, I was somewhat taken aback. I wondered how anyone (especially a priest) could speak about the irrelevance of prayer. After all, isn't any type of prayer always relevant? So I couldn't wait to read the chapters to see what Father Green meant. When I had finished reading both chapters, I discovered his meaning.

Father Green explains that prayer is irrelevant when it is merely our attempt to get God to do what we want — to get God to do our will. On the other hand, prayer is very relevant when it is our attempt to discover what God wants of us and our attempt to seek the strength to carry out his will.

If our primary goal in prayer is to let God know our needs and to ask him to take care of them, we run the risk of developing a kind of professional relationship with God, not a personal one. We will see God simply as one who can take care of some of our needs. When we go to see a professional person — let's say our doctor — we are just interested in the services that he can render to us. We are not there to develop a personal relationship with him. It is different with people we call friends. We do not visit them primarily to take care of some business. Rather, we visit with them so that we can deepen our friendship. We may listen to them, they may listen to us, or we may simply enjoy each other's presence. In other words, the primary focus is not to obtain a service but to deepen a friendship.

The Lord wants us to regard him as a friend with whom we would want to "waste time," someone to whom we willingly listen (see John 15:15 and Matthew 11:28-30). It would be sad if we treated God as a "Divine Do-gooder" whom we called on only in time of need. If we are to develop a personal relationship with the Lord, we must be willing not only to open our hearts to God about our needs but also to sit quietly at the feet of the Master so that he can speak to us (see Luke 10:38-42).

HOW GOD SPEAKS TO US

Presuming we are interested in making prayer a time when we primarily listen for the voice of God, our question might be, ''How does God speak to us?'' After all, no one has ever seen God or heard his voice the way we have heard the voice of friends. God uses many channels to speak his Word to us. He speaks to us through sunrises and sunsets, through a smiling face, through sickness patiently endured, through the needy beggar. He speaks to us especially through sacred writings, through the lives of other people, through the events of daily life, and through his creation. This can be seen in the following personal examples.

Through sacred writings: God can speak through a sacred or inspired text. Recall the Gospel for the Feast of All Saints which focuses on the Beatitudes (see Matthew 5:1-12). In pondering and dwelling on this text for a few minutes, I could practically hear the Lord saying to me, ''Saints are people who live the Beatitudes. They don't just read about them or tell others about them. They actually live each Beatitude.'' I especially felt the Lord say to me, ''Saints are, above all, single-minded in their approach to life. They seek me above and in all things.'' This was a simple but beautiful message which encouraged me to be more vigilant in my seeking of God. The next time I read this text God may say something different to me, for the Word of God is inexhaustible.

Through the lives of other people: God can speak through the words of other people or through the quiet witness of their lives. I live next door to a community of Sisters who are well-known for their hospitality. Not only do they welcome and feed the people of the parish whom they know, but they also welcome and feed strangers whom they do not know. Through the Sisters' love for people, God sends a message to me about the importance of hospitality in the Christian life.

Through the events of daily life: God can and does speak through the events of daily life. A few years ago while driving on an interstate highway, my car skidded on the wet road and crashed into a wall. I was very fortunate that I did not injure either myself or anyone else. Without reflecting on the event, I could simply have said, ''Boy, I was pretty lucky,'' and then proceeded to see about the repair of my car. But by prayerfully reflecting on the event, it was as if God said to me: "Eamon, you need to drive more carefully on wet roads. This should remind you of how fragile and vulnerable human life is. The best way to thank me for the daily gift of life is to live it fully but with proper caution." Although I heard God say this to me, he might have spoken a different message to someone else in the same situation.

Through God's creation: God can speak to us through the majesty and beauty of his creation. Elizabeth Barrett Browning, in her poem entitled *Aurora Leigh,* puts it this way:

> Earth's crammed with heaven,
> And every common bush afire with God;
> But only he who sees takes off his shoes;
> The rest sit round it and pluck blackberries.

In Cocoa Beach, Florida, I live one block from the Atlantic Ocean. It is difficult to walk the beach and not see in it a reflection of the Creator. The big, mighty waves of the ocean hurrying toward the seashore and the lovely sunrises speak to me of the power, the majesty, and the beauty of God.

Such "reading into" or interpreting the events and encounters of life might seem rather strange to some people, yet to the person of faith it is perfectly normal. The eighteenth-century spiritual director, Jean-Pierre de Caussade, in his book, *Abandonment to Divine Providence,* writes:

> There is never a moment when God does not come forward in the guise of some suffering or some duty, and all that takes place within, around us, and through us both includes and hides his activity. . . . If we could lift the veil and if we watched with vigilant attention, God would endlessly reveal himself to us. . . . It is faith which interprets God for us. Without its light we should not even know that God was speaking but would hear only the confused, meaningless babble of creatures. As Moses saw the flame of fire in the bush and heard the voice of God coming from it, so faith will enable us to understand his hidden signs, so that amidst all the apparent clutter and disorder we shall see all the loveliness and perfection of divine wisdom.

Now we may ask how we know that we are hearing God's voice and not just hearing or reading into events what we want to hear or read. This certainly is an important question because we humans have quite a facility for making God say to us what we want him to say. This question has been dealt with in Chapter Three of the booklet, *Help for Making Difficult Decisions* (Liguori Publications), where several practical steps are recommended to help us discern the voice of God from other voices.

Learning to hear and discern the voice of God is both a gift and an art. It is a gift of the Holy Spirit which we need to receive frequently and an art to learn by trial and error (see 1 Corinthians 12:10). Getting to know the voice of God is somewhat like getting to know the voice of a newfound friend. At first we do not readily recognize our friend's voice on the phone. But as the friendship grows we recognize the person's voice as soon as we hear the word "Hi." If we live our lives in the company of Jesus, we will become more and more familiar with his voice. (Later in this book when we discuss the Prayer of Consciousness Examen, we will consider another excellent way to grow in our ability to hear, discern, and respond to the voice of our God.

REFLECTION QUESTIONS

1. What insight in these pages made the greatest impression on you?
2. Some people act as if God speaks to them constantly. How do you react to such people? Does God speak to you? Can you give an example?
3. If you have grown recently in your ability to hear and discern God's voice, what has facilitated this new growth? What still hinders you from being a better hearer of God's voice?
4. Did you disagree with or have trouble understanding any part of this section?
5. After doing the suggested prayer exercise that follows, describe your experience.

SUGGESTED PRAYER EXERCISE

Tomorrow make a special effort to be attentive to any messages that God may wish to send you through reading, persons, events, or creation. At the end of the day take a minute or two to jot down the messages you think you received from God.

PART TWO

SPECIFIC PRAYER STYLES

At times authors make the mistake of urging people to pray without offering them any suggestions or guidelines on how they can spend quiet time with the Lord. It's like urging people to swim and assuming that they know how to go about it.

Part One examined the four keys to effective prayer and demonstrated how these fundmentals are extremely important to every prayer life. Part Two will explore some specific styles of praying.

Before looking at specific prayer styles, it is important to keep in mind some pertinent facts about prayer styles in general.

Each person has to discover the rhythm that best suits his or her personality and spiritual needs. Saint John of the Cross writes: "God leads each one along different paths so that hardly one spirit will be found like another in even half its method or procedure." The sixteenth-century Spanish mystic reserves some of his harshest criticisms for spiritual directors who insist on one and only one style of prayer for every person they direct. In a way, learning to pray and using different styles of praying are somewhat similar to buying and using different pairs of shoes.

First of all, we don't usually think about wearing shoes that already belong to someone else.

Second, when we go to the shoe store we usually end up trying on several styles and sizes of shoes until we discover the pair that fits us best.

Third, most people buy different kinds of shoes for different occasions.

Fourth, we may buy a pair of shoes that we don't particularly like and that don't even fit very well, yet these shoes eventually may become one of our favorite pairs.

In a similar way, this is true of our prayer life.

First: We should not try to pray in a particular way just because this way works for or fits someone else.

Second: We should try several prayer styles until we discover the ones that best suit our temperament, spiritual needs, and schedules.

Third: It is wise to be familiar with a variety of prayer styles that we can use at different times.

Fourth: We may sometimes find ourselves feeling very comfortable with a prayer style that initially felt very awkward for us.

Like shoes, prayer styles are a means to an end; therefore, we should use them in a way that best serves our needs. During any of our daily prayer periods we may use several prayer styles.

The prayer styles that I will discuss in Part Two are not necessarily the most important ones, nor are they treated in any kind of hierarchy of importance. Basically they are prayer styles that I use and that are comfortable for me in varying degrees. I have omitted those that I either haven't "tried on for fit" or have tried but found that they don't work very well for me. I have confined myself to a selection of prayer styles that I have personally experienced and that I have found helpful. I hope the readers will find some suggestions that may, in some way, enrich their prayer life.

1
PRAYER
OF THANKSGIVING

Ten were cleansed, were they not? Where are the other nine? Has none but this foreigner returned to give thanks to God?

(Luke 17:17-18)

Father, all powerful and ever-living God,
we do well always and everywhere to give you thanks.
You have no need of our praise,
yet our desire to thank you is itself your gift.
Our prayer of thanksgiving adds nothing to your greatness,
but makes us grow in your grace,
through Jesus Christ our Lord.

(Mass Preface, Weekday IV)

In the prayer of thanksgiving we give gratitude to God for his loving activity in creation, in the lives of others, and in our own lives. The words of the preface indicate that God has no need of our thanks in the way that we need stroking and affirmation. Yet we can safely assume that our prayers and deeds of thanks do please God. Even more, we know that developing a grateful heart toward God is beneficial to our mental and spiritual well-being. When we take time out to recognize and give thanks to God for what is good in life, we not only recognize God as the Source of all good things, but we also grow in our experience of God as a loving and generous Person. In turn, this experience of God will probably lead us to a more generous giving of ourselves to God. In short, our acts of gratitude to God deepen our relationship with God — hence, the vital importance of taking time out for the prayer of thanksgiving.

We show extreme ingratitude when we take little or no time to identify God's gifts or blessings and rarely give thanks. Worse still, we may believe that the blessings in life are just the result of our own hard work and ingenuity. Moses sternly warned the Israelites not to have that attitude toward the blessings of God. He tells them:

> You then become haughty of heart and unmindful of the LORD, your God, who brought you out of the land of Egypt, that place of slavery; who guided you through the vast and terrible desert . . . who . . . fed you in the desert with manna. . . . Otherwise, you might say to yourselves, ''It is my own power and the strength of my own hand that has obtained for me this wealth.'' Remember then, it is the LORD, your God, who gives you the power to acquire wealth.
>
> (Deuteronomy 8:14-18)

Moses is reminding the Israelites never to forget the gratitude they owe to the one who is the Source of their blessings. When we take little or no time out to give thanks to God, we may begin to think that God is more or less absent from our lives. When we lose the connection between God and the good things in life we run the risk of losing our relationship with God — period. We will perceive God as distant and uninvolved in our lives.

The prayer of thanksgiving not only enhances our relationship with God, but it also helps our own general sense of well-being. The grateful person is usually a happy person, and the grumbling person is usually unhappy. The priest/sociologist, Andrew Greeley, in his book, *The Bottom-Line Catechism,* writes:

> The empirical research my colleagues and I have done confirms the age-old Christian tradition that prayers of gratitude are the most important, for the relationship between prayer and mental health and marital satisfaction seems to be true only for those whose frequent prayers are prayers of thanksgiving. Prayer brings psychological peace and personal happiness precisely insofar as it becomes a grateful response to a gift of love that is perceived as having already been given.

World-famous catechist, Jesuit Father Johannes Hofinger, in his book, *Pastoral Life in the Power of the Spirit,* has written:

Lack of gratitude is always a clear sign of selfishness, and selfishness is the hotbed of all kinds of emotional disturbances. Genuine, deep gratitude, on the other hand, opens man in a healthy way toward others; it always helps him to overcome an unhealthy concentration upon himself and it has, by its very nature, a tremendous power of interior healing.

All of this impresses on us the importance of developing a grateful spirit and shows us the potential destructiveness of an ungrateful spirit. A spirit of gratefulness deepens our relationship with God; it increases our mental well-being and helps us to be happier people.

Saint Paul exhorts us: "Rejoice always. Pray without ceasing. In all circumstances give thanks" (1 Thessalonians 5:16-18). Does this mean that we are supposed to thank God for the painful and evil things that happen to us? Surely God does not expect or want us to give thanks for the evil things that happen to us or others. But we can and should thank God for his presence and help in times of evil and pain. We can also give thanks to God for the way he is able to bring good out of evil. No doubt all of us can tell stories of how God turned the tables on evil and used the event to teach us some valuable lesson or bring us closer to him.

In all this we need to be aware that one danger in this form of prayer is repression of unpleasant emotions. We may first need to grieve the losses we suffer or feel and then express our feelings of anger and frustration before we praise God and open our hearts to the joy and peace that this brings with it. (Jesuit Father John Wright, in Chapter Four of his book, *A Theology of Christian Prayer,* provides further insights on the theology of the prayer of thanksgiving.)

How then should we give thanks to God for his blessings? We can do this in countless ways. Here are a few suggestions.

- The Mass is the great prayer of thanksgiving for Catholic Christians. The word *Eucharist* means thanksgiving. We can attend a weekday Mass and use it as our prayer of thanksgiving for some particular blessing in our lives.
- We can use the five decades of the rosary to give thanks to God for five specific blessings in our lives. It can't be emphasized

enough how important it is to actually name what we think are the blessings in our lives.

- We can give thanks by sharing our blessings with others. For example, we could thank the Lord for the blessing of health by becoming a blood donor or by visiting the sick or shut-ins of our community. We could thank the Lord for material blessings by sharing those blessings with the poor.
- As we walk through any given day, we can whisper or shout aloud a word of thanks to the Lord.
- We can also compose a personal litany of the things we are grateful for in life.

REFLECTION QUESTIONS

1. What insight in these pages made the greatest impression on you?
2. What do you feel most grateful for in life?
3. In your experience, how true is it to say that the practice of thanking God for specific gifts leads to a greater sense of God's love and presence in your life and helps you to be a happier person?
4. Have you ever tried to thank God for the hardships — even the evil happenings — in your life? If so, how was that experience? If not, what are your thoughts or feelings about doing that?
5. Did you disagree with or have trouble understanding any part of this section?
6. After doing the suggested prayer exercise that follows, describe your experience.

SUGGESTED PRAYER EXERCISE

Make a list of the good things in life that you are grateful for and that you may be inclined to take for granted. Also try to get in touch with some events in your present life for which you would find it very hard to be grateful. Try to give thanks to God for *all* the happenings in your life, trusting that as you reach beyond your feelings, God will bless you.

2
PRAYER
OF PETITION

And I tell you, ask and you will receive; seek and you will find; knock and the door will be opened to you. . . . If you then, who are wicked, know how to give good gifts to your children, how much more will the Father in heaven give the holy Spirit to those who ask him?

(Luke 11:9,13)

The power of prayer to obtain graces does not depend on our merits but on the mercy of God. But the graces that we ask for must be graces related to our eternal welfare. We may ask for temporal goods, but they must be asked for only on the condition that they will be of benefit to our souls.

(Saint Alphonsus Liguori)

For most of us the prayer of petition is not only the most common but also the most intriguing and mysterious of all types of prayer. We probably have several questions about how this prayer works. We may wonder why we have the prayer of petition — period. Doesn't God know what we need? Why should we offer him any suggestions on how to improve people and the world in which we live? In the prayer of petition are we trying to clue God in on what he might otherwise have overlooked? Does our prayer of petition move God to do things that he otherwise had not planned to do? Why did Jesus heal the son of the widow of Nain immediately (see Luke 7:11-17) and wait for twenty years or so to answer Saint Monica's prayer for the conversion of her son Augustine? Why does God seemingly not answer some prayers — for example, those for the healing of a young mother who eventually dies of cancer? On the lighter side, we might ask: "What does God do when the Miami Dolphins are playing a football game against the Dallas Cowboys and the fans of both teams are praying that their team wins?''

Trying to explain the nature of petitionary prayer and how it works is a theological problem to which there is no satisfactory answer. In groping with this problem, we are trying to understand the ways of God and how God works in our world. Saint Paul realizes the complexity of this question and writes: ''Oh, the depth of the riches and wisdom and knowledge of God! How inscrutable are his judgments and how unsearchable his ways! For who has known the mind of the Lord?'' (Romans 11:33-34). For most — if not all — of the great theologians and saints who have struggled with questions about how petitionary prayer works, the bottom line is similar to that of Job who finally admitted his inability to solve the mystery of suffering. He told the Lord that he had been trying to solve things too big for him (see Job 40:3-5).

Yet it is legitimate for the curious-minded among us to probe the mystery of petitionary prayer so that we can live with it a little more intelligently and a little less anxiously. One helpful insight comes from an article by William Whalen in a September, 1983, *U.S. Catholic* article entitled ''How Catholic Prayer Became a Mass Movement'':

> The prayer of petition is part of God's plan for man. When we say that God answers prayers we do not mean that prayer can cause God to change his mind. God has made the whole world and governs it with his providence. Everything that occurs in the world takes place according to his plan. But it is part of God's plan that certain gifts will be given to man only in answer to prayer. We pray not to change God's plans, but in order to receive from God those things which he has planned to give us in answer to our prayers.

Our daily experiences seem to bear out the basic truth of this statement. There are some gifts we give to others without their asking. Other gifts we give only when we are asked. In waiting to act in response to our prayers or until we petition him, God is allowing us to participate in our own salvation and the salvation of others. Also, the purpose of petitionary prayer is not to inform God of our needs but rather to inform ourselves. Petitionary prayer deepens our awareness of how much we need God at every moment of our lives. When we pray in this way, we can always expect some change in ourselves if not in the external circumstances which prompted our prayer. We can always expect God to give us the strength to deal with the circumstances of our lives even if he does not change them. This seemingly was the experience of the author of Psalm 138, who writes:

> When I called, you answered me;
> you built up strength within me.
>
> (Psalm 138:3)

What the psalmist is telling us is that ''having God answer our prayers'' sometimes involves ''having him build up his strength'' in us. While we may not understand the how of petitionary prayer, we should have no doubt about its importance. God does want us to express our petitions, and he does answer these prayers, even if not in the exact way we wanted. The *Our Father,* the prayer Jesus taught his disciples, is basically a prayer of petition, particularly the second part of it. Many verses in the psalms also express belief in the prayer of petition:

> Blessed be the LORD,
> for he has heard the sound of my pleading.
>
> (Psalm 28:6)

> When I call out to the LORD,
> he answers me from his holy mountain.
>
> (Psalm 3:5)

We should never become so sophisticated in our spiritual life that we feel petitionary prayer is beneath us. Thinking this would imply that we have outgrown our need for God. We will always need the prayer of petition because we will always need to express our dependence on God. Of course, as we mature in prayer and learn to trust more in God's inscrutable ways, our attitude toward petitionary prayer will change. It will become more God-centered and less self-centered.

PROPER ATTITUDES
FOR PETITIONARY PRAYER

There are two important attitudes to bring to the prayer of petition. We must be aware that God is certainly interested in our prayer, and we must realize that the primary purpose of the prayer of petition is to deepen our relationship with God.

Awareness of God's interest: When we petition God in prayer, we are not trying to contact Someone who already has a full "case load" and is therefore just not interested in "another case." God is present, active, and intensely interested in all of his creation. He is the origin (and the sustainer) of all things, drawing and guiding all to their Omega point. Creation — of which we are a part — is God's big project. God is passionately concerned that it evolves and develops according to his plan. About this plan Saint Paul tells us:

> He chose us in him, before the foundation of the world, to be holy and without blemish before him. In love he destined us for adoption to himself through Jesus Christ. . . . he has made known to us the mystery of his will in accord with his favor that he set forth in him as a plan for the fullness of times, to sum up all things in Christ, in heaven and on earth.
>
> (Ephesians 1:4-5, 9-10)

In our vulnerable and weak moments we may doubt and even disbelieve God's interest in creation. Often it may seem to us that God is on a "long vacation," is "off duty," or is frequently "out to lunch." When we think such human thoughts, we should reinforce our faith with the knowledge that God has already proved his passionate interest in the most radical way possible — through the life, death, and Resurrection of Jesus. "No one has greater love than this, to lay down one's life for one's friends" (John 15:13). Perhaps the best proof of God's love for us is that "while we were still sinners Christ died for us" (Romans 5:8). Hence, the burden is not on God to prove his interest in us; the burden is on us to believe in a truth that has already been proven in no uncertain way. This truth is very important for us to believe when it comes to prayer. It should help us to relax and gently make known our needs to God, trusting in his interest just as we would trust in the interest of a good friend.

Realization of our primary purpose: A closer relationship with God is the primary purpose of our petitionary prayer. The

Garden of Gethsemane was the scene of Jesus' prayer of petition. In Mark 14:36, Jesus asked his Father to preserve his life, to "take this cup away from me" — a very legitimate request. Yet one thing was of greater priority for Jesus — his relationship with his Father. He came to do his Father's will: "Not what I will but what you will" (Mark 14:36).

Behind every prayer of petition — or every prayer for that matter — should be the fundamental request that our prayer may, above all else, deepen our relationship with God. When we view the prayer of petition in this way, we can say that no prayer goes unanswered. Every prayer of petition should be viewed in the context of our overall relationship with God. The implication is that our prayers of petition ought to be viewed in terms of how they will affect our relationship with God.

For example, if we seek a better salary — a legitimate desire — we should be concerned that extra funds will not diminish our relationship with God or make us less sensitive to the poor. If we pray for an advancement in our careers, we need to keep in mind that in God's design such an advancement may not help our relationship with him or be good for our family life. While it is legitimate to pray to God for what is good in life, we should always see such benefits in the larger context of how they will affect our relationship with God — the greatest good of all. On the spiritual journey the only absolute good is God and his will; all else, even health, is relative to our relationship with him. As we become more mature pray-ers we should seek and praise God's holy will and submit to it unconditionally. Such an attitude will be our greatest help in dealing with so-called unanswered prayer.

A contrary attitude is found in those who are *merely* concerned about obtaining what they want — with little or no concern about how these desires might affect their relationship with God. When people seek physical healing at a healing service, we sometimes see examples of this attitude. They may receive the physical healing, but their spiritual relationship with God remains unchanged. Their main focus is on the gift to be received and not on God the great giver. There is interest in the giver only insofar as that one has the capacity to give what the seeker wants. To summarize: When we take our requests to God, our overriding concern should be how the granting or the denial of such requests affects our relationship with the Lord.

WHAT TO
PRAY FOR

First: We should pray that our primary concern is God and our fidelity to the will of God. All else is relative and it need not be our concern. "Incline my heart according to your will, O Lord" is a prayer that frequently should be on our lips. In praying this prayer of petition we are asking God to draw our whole being into line with his plan for us.

Second: We should pray that God will help each of us to become the unique and original person we were created to be. Each person is created to be a unique manifestation of God's truth, goodness, and beauty in the world. Our deepest and most authentic fulfillment in life is discovering and becoming that unique person. Here our prayer should be something like this: "Lord, help me to discover and become the self you created me to be, and help me to resist any temptation to try to be a carbon copy of anyone else."

Third: Since all of us have a particular vocation in life (married, religious, single) and a particular career with duties and responsibilities, we certainly should pray frequently that God will help us to be faithful to our particular vocation and duties in life. This means responding to the daily challenges of our life situation in a creative and positive way — and this, despite the temptation to withdraw and say "no" to the duties and challenges of life.

Fourth: We should pray for our specific needs. Some kind of a "prayer list" — which can be lengthened or shortened at our convenience — can be used on a regular basis. Here is a sample of such a list:

- "Father, help me to discover and embrace your will at all times."
- "Father, help me to discover and become the person you created me to be."
- "Jesus, lead me into a deeper experience of the Father's love for me."
- "Jesus, fill my heart with your love for the people you have given me to lead and to serve."

- "Holy Spirit, help me to use well the gifts of time, treasure and talent that you have given me."
- "Holy Spirit, reveal to me the sin and woundedness that hinder me from surrendering myself more fully to you."

If this list seems rather self-centered, it is because petitionary prayer is prayer for self as opposed to intercessory prayer which is prayer for others.

As the Lord answers very specific prayers, we grow in our conviction about the value of petitionary prayer. We may even write down in our spiritual journals the Lord's answers to special requests. In our prayers of petition we should always say, "Lord, help me to recognize your answer to my prayer." Sometimes we are blind to the Lord's answer because we are locked into wanting God to answer our prayer in a very specific way.

To summarize: It is interesting to note that our requests in prayer can reveal much about our images of God and self and our relationship with God. For example, if we don't dare pray for the seemingly impossible things in life, is it because we think that God can't handle such a request? If we rarely make small requests such as "Lord, help me to find a parking space," is it because we have an image of God which causes us to think God would be too busy to have an interest in our parking problem? If we rarely pray for ourselves because we think it is selfish, does this outlook reveal a poor self-image? Do we think that we don't deserve God's attention? If our prayer is primarily dominated by petitionary prayer, what might this say about our relationship with God? If we throw temper tantrums when God doesn't respond to our prayer exactly as we asked, what does this reveal about us and about how we relate to God?

REFLECTION QUESTIONS

1. What insight in these pages made the greatest impression on you?
2. According to God's plan, certain gifts are given only in answer to prayer. Have you experienced this in your life?
3. Are you convinced that God is interested in your personal prayers?

4. Review the section in this chapter on *What to Pray For*. What has been your experience in these areas?
5. Did you disagree with or have trouble understanding any part of this section?
6. After doing the suggested prayer exercise that follows, describe your experience.

SUGGESTED PRAYER EXERCISE

Draw up for yourself a prayer list — one that expresses the desires of your heart in relationship to God, family, neighbor, self, work, and the larger world.

3
PRAYER
OF PETITION
(Continued)

O LORD, hear my prayer;
    hearken to my pleading in your
        faithfulness;
    in your justice answer me.

(Psalm 143:1)

Jesus Christ has promised that whatever we ask the Father in his
name, the Father will give us. But he does so, always with the
understanding that we ask under the proper conditions.

(Saint Alphonsus Liguori)

A very definite cause of alienation from and frustration with
God is that we sometimes perceive him as uncaring because he
doesn't answer our prayers. This is particularly true when our
requests are very close to our heart — such as holding a marriage
together, healing a parent of cancer, and similar problems. There
does not seem to be a definite or perfect answer to the problem of
unanswered prayer, but it is possible to offer some insights on this
difficult question. Barbara Gawle, in her book, *How to Pray*,
describes the conditions that interfere with our prayers. She
maintains that some of our prayers remain unanswered because the
spiritual circuit between ourselves and God somehow becomes
broken. This can be seen from our viewpoint (the ways we block
communication with God) and from God's viewpoint (the way
God in his wisdom views the situation). (Much of what follows has
been gleaned from Barbara Gawle's book.)

FOUR REASONS
WHY OUR PRAYERS
GO UNANSWERED

Obviously, there are countless reasons why — from the human viewpoint — our prayers go unanswered. Here, however, are four standard ones to which we can all relate.

We pray with an unforgiving heart. The little boy who prayed, "Forgive us our trash baskets as we forgive those who put their trash in our baskets," had the wrong words but the right idea. When we put our trash in other people's baskets, we not only alienate ourselves from them but also from God who loves them very much. In Mark, Jesus proclaims, "When you stand to pray, forgive anyone against whom you have a grievance . . . " (Mark 11:25). In Matthew, he says, "If you bring your gift to the altar, and there recall that your brother has anything against you, leave your gift there at the altar, go first and be reconciled with your brother, and then come and offer your gift" (Matthew 5:23-24). These sayings of Jesus clearly point out how important it is to go to God with a forgiving heart, or at least with a heart that desires to forgive.

We ask wrongly. "You ask but do not receive, because you ask wrongly" (James 4:3). What are some examples of asking wrongly? We might, for example, pray for a job and not get it. The reason for this is not God but the simple fact that we don't have the skills needed for the job. Again, suppose we ask God to get us through a particular test. We fail the test and get upset with God. The reason we failed, though, was that we didn't study the subject matter sufficiently. When our prayers seem to fall on "deaf ears," we might ask if our action — or lack thereof — caused the problem.

We lack faith and persistence. Deep down we may not really believe that God is interested in our request and that he wants to help us. Or perhaps we ask for something one time and fail to persevere in prayer. Saint Monica had to pray many years before her son Augustine turned to God.

We fail to do our part. Failure to do our part is another reason why our prayers go unanswered. We might pray for reconciliation of a particular conflict but be unwilling to admit our own wrong in the relationship. We ask God to bless our worship service but we do little or nothing to prepare for the service by creating the kind of conditions that facilitate God's action. While God sometimes helps us when we can't help ourselves, he certainly expects us to help ourselves (and others) when possible. As the old saying goes, "We must pray as if all depended on God and act as if all depended on ourselves."

TWO REASONS WHY GOD
DOESN'T ALWAYS ANSWER
OUR PRAYERS

Besides the four human reasons for unanswered prayer, there are divine reasons for God not answering our prayers. Here are two general reasons that can help us understand our unanswered prayers.

God's ways are not always our ways. In the Book of Isaiah, God tells us, "My thoughts are not your thoughts, nor are your ways my ways" (Isaiah 55:8). In the ebb and flow of our lives, God sometimes "writes straight with crooked lines" or works in strange ways. What might seem to be a "No" to us might be a "Yes" from God. God may deny our literal request but actually grant us the deeper, perhaps unconscious, desires of our heart. We may have a particular goal we wish to attain, and we may have ideas about how to attain it. God may help us to reach our goal but in ways we never thought of.

Father Basil Pennington, in his *Ways of Prayer,* writes:

> God will give us whatever we want, asking in prayer — what we truly want, not what we say we want or even think we want. God listens to the heart, not to the lips. He knows, too, how limited is our understanding and knowledge. He sees our truest desires and knows how they can best be fulfilled. And this is what he grants. We may not see it at the moment, but we will in time. . . . If God seems to be saying "No" to some prayers, it is because he is saying "Yes" to the deepest prayer of our hearts.

When Saint Paul asked God to take away his thorn in the flesh, God said, "No," but only in order that he could say "Yes" to a deeper desire of Paul — namely, to experience the power of God in his being (see 2 Corinthians 12:7-10). A second example of how God sometimes says "No" to one request of ours so that he can say "Yes" to a deeper request is found in the prayer of a man whose wife was killed in an accident. And although his daughter also died, and he himself went blind, he was still able to address God in this magnificent way:

> I asked for health,
> so that I could do great things for you.
> You gave me sickness,
> so that I could do greater things.
> I asked for riches,
> so that I could be happy.
> You gave me poverty,
> so that I could be really wise.
> I asked for strength,
> so that I could fight for you.
> You gave me weakness,
> so that I could rely on you.
> I got none of the things I asked for,
> but all the things I hoped for.
> (Author Unknown)

God's timing differs from our timing. God's timing may not be ours, so we may think that God is refusing our prayer. Eventually, however, we have to admit that God knew best after all.

A few years ago I had a personal experience of the wisdom and giftedness of God's timing in contrast to mine. In October, 1985, while residing in another parish, I applied to become pastor of my present parish. Once I had made my formal request I was anxious, for various reasons, to move as soon as possible. According to the normal way that personnel changes happen in our diocese, I should have been in my new parish by the end of October. In actuality, due to certain circumstances, my appointment was not formalized until the middle of December. I found the waiting period to be very difficult. It was not easy to continue functioning in one place when my mind and emotions were already someplace else.

During these same weeks I was engaged in writing the first draft of this book — a stage of writing that demanded much time and concentration as I tried to collect materials from many different sources. So, while I waited for my new appointment I had more time than usual to write. As each week went by, I found myself in the paradoxical and humorous position of feeling frustrated with God for not making my transfer happen faster but also feeling very grateful to him for the time I had to collect resource materials for each new section of the book.

I was particularly grateful when I realized that I would have much less time to write as I became more and more involved in my new parish. If God had moved according to my schedule, I might never have completed this book, or I certainly would not have finished it as soon as I did.

The bottom line in all of this involves growing in the ability to trust in Divine Providence and to trust that he is working out all things for the best (see Romans 8:28). A poem, "The Weaver," beautifully sums up all that has been said here about God's ways and our ways:

> My life is but a weaving
> Between my Lord and me.
> I cannot choose the colors
> He worketh steadily.
> Offtimes He weaveth sorrow,
> And I in foolish pride
> Forget He sees the upper,
> And I, the underside.
> Not till the loom is silent
> And the shuttles cease to fly,
> Shall God unroll the canvas
> And explain the reason why
> The dark threads are as needful
> In the Weaver's skillful hand
> As the threads of gold and silver
> In the pattern He has planned.
>   (Author Unknown)

REFLECTION QUESTIONS

1. What insight in these pages made the greatest impression on you?

2. Have you ever had the experience when "God's timing" was better than your own?

3. What helps you to deal with the problem of unanswered prayer?

4. Recall a recent example of God answering your prayer. Was it answered in the exact way you asked?

5. Did you disagree with or have trouble understanding any part of this section?

6. After doing the suggested prayer exercise that follows, describe your experience.

SUGGESTED PRAYER EXERCISE

Relive in your imagination a specific time in your life when — thanks to God's timing — you did not receive what you had fervently prayed for. Talk about this with God.

4
PRAYER
OF INTERCESSION

First of all, then, I ask that supplications, prayers, petitions, and thanksgivings be offered for everyone, for kings and for all in authority, that we may lead a quiet and tranquil life in all devotion and dignity. This is good and pleasing to God our savior, who wills everyone to be saved and to come to knowledge of the truth.

(1 Timothy 2:1-4)

It is only at the end of this world that we shall realize how the destinies of persons and nations have been shaped, not so much by the external actions of powerful men and by events that seemed inevitable, but by the quiet, silent, irresistible prayer of persons the world will never know.

(Anthony de Mello, S.J.)

The prayer of intercession is our prayer for other people and their needs. Sacred Scripture has several stories and images of individuals interceding before God for others. For example, the Book of Exodus relates how Moses frequently interceded before God for his people. A lovely example of this shows Moses pleading with God on behalf of his unfaithful people:

But Moses implored the LORD, his God, saying, "Why, O LORD, should your wrath blaze up against your own people, whom you brought out of the land of Egypt with such great power and with so strong a hand? Why should the Egyptians say, 'With evil intent he brought them out, that he might kill them in the mountains and exterminate them from the face of the earth'? Let your blazing wrath die down; relent in punishing your people. Remember your servants Abraham, Isaac and Israel, and how you swore to them by your own self, saying, 'I will make your descendants as numerous as the stars in the sky; and all this land that I promised, I will give your descendants as their perpetual heritage.' '' So the LORD relented in the punishment he had threatened to inflict on his people.

(Exodus 32:11-14)

There are also many examples of intercessory prayers in the New Testament. In the Cana story, we see Mary interceding for a young couple (see John 2:1-12). In Matthew 8:5-13, the Roman centurion intercedes with Jesus on behalf of his sick servant. In Luke 19:41-44, Jesus weeps over Jerusalem, crying out for her conversion.

Through this type of prayer we, in a spirit of solidarity, enter into the pain of others and go before the throne of God on their behalf. Father Pennington, in *Ways of Prayer,* writes: ''Intercessory prayer is not a question of a lot of prayers; it is a question of a lot of love. He or she who loves much accomplishes much when that love is coupled with strong faith.''

By means of intercessory prayer we join with Jesus who ''lives forever'' to intercede for all who come to God through him (see Hebrews 7:25). As baptized persons sharing in the priesthood of Christ, we are all called to join Jesus' ministry of intercession. In the spirit of Mary at Cana we bring the hurts, the pain, and the needs of our brothers and sisters to Jesus, trusting, like Mary, that he will do something.

Several years ago I had the opportunity to spend a few days at Bethany House of Intercession in Providence, Rhode Island, a house of prayer run by a group of priests whose main ministry is to intercede continuously for priests throughout the world. Priests from all over the world visited this house of prayer. Each time a newcomer arrived the group would gather around him and pray that God would grant him the gifts of intercession, listening, and compassion.

Even though many of the priests who came to Bethany House were heavily burdened with personal problems, they were asked upon entry to focus on the burdens of others rather than their own burdens, trusting that as they reached out in compassion to others God would take care of their needs. Invariably they all found that while being concerned with the needs of others, God quietly took care of their needs.

All were asked to pray specifically for priests with problems and struggles similar to their own (discouragement, depression, worry, alcoholism, anger, or whatever). After several days of praying for a priest with a problem similar to their own, most of them received the healing they needed. The priests discovered that their own wounds were touched and healed as they learned, through intercessory prayer, how much Jesus loved another person who was just like themselves. Those who devote themselves to the ministry of healing know this quite well. The Jesuit priests, Matthew and Dennis Linn (together with Sheila Fabricant), in their book, *A Course on Healing Life's Hurts*, have this to say: "The easiest way to receive healing is to pray for someone who is just like ourselves and to pray with the deep compassion of Jesus."

WAYS OF INTERCEDING

What are some forms of intercession or ways to intercede for other people? The prayer list to which I referred earlier also contains a list of names and concerns that I wish to bring before the Lord in intercession. Usually I just go through the list, mentioning each person or concern and asking God to take care of the situation. Sometimes I'll use the rosary as a way to pray.

The authors of *Prayer Course in Healing Life's Hurts* have several suggestions for intercessory prayer:

- Choose something you often struggle with (for example, envy, anxiety, some physical ailment, or other difficulty) and intercede for someone with a similar struggle.
- Read the newspaper and intercede for one person whose difficulties are recorded there.
- Stand in the place of another and receive the Eucharist for him or her.
- Like the centurion in Luke 7:1-10, bring someone to Jesus and ask for healing. Try to see that person with the eyes of Jesus and strive to feel Jesus' compassion for him or her. Once you are filled with the compassion of Jesus, see yourself laying your hand upon that person and see that person filled with light and strength as you breathe Jesus's life into him or her.

One elderly lady says she has a big bushel basket, and when people ask for prayers, she just "throws their petitions into the bushel basket," trusting that God will take care of them.

Intercession can also be done in a group. For example, some couples gather together to pray for God's blessing, strength, and protection on their marriages. Others gather to pray for the spiritual renewal of the parish and for people who are struggling in any way.

As with the prayer of petition, we have no guarantee that our prayers of intercession will be answered exactly as we want. Not everyone Jesus prayed for was changed. "He was not able to perform any mighty deed there [his own part of the country], apart from curing a few sick people by laying his hands on them. He was amazed at their lack of faith" (Mark 6:5-6). While we can't guarantee that the people we pray for will be changed, we can be sure that *we* will be changed.

REFLECTION QUESTIONS

1. What insight in these pages made the greatest impression on you?
2. "The easiest way to receive healing is to pray for someone who is just like ourselves and to pray with the deep compassion of Jesus." What are your thoughts on this suggestion?
3. Which of the suggestions for intercessory prayer in this chapter appeal to you most?
4. What is usually the focus of your intercessory prayer? Can you give an example of God responding to a specific prayer of intercession?
5. Did you disagree with or have trouble understanding any part of this section?
6. After doing the suggested prayer exercise that follows, describe your experience.

SUGGESTED PRAYER EXERCISE

Choose something you often struggle with and begin to intercede for someone with a similar struggle. This is most beneficial if you have a specific person in mind.

5
PRAYER
OF CONTRITION

If we say, "We are without sin," we deceive ourselves, and the truth is not in us. If we acknowledge our sins, he is faithful and just and will forgive our sins and cleanse us from every wrongdoing.

(1 John 1:8-9)

We must be sorry for our sinfulness. Sorrow is the fruit of love. When we realize God's overwhelming love for us in spite of our past refusal to accept his love, how can we help but respond in love?

(David E. Rosage)

The words of the First Letter of Saint John quoted above assure us not only of the reality of sin but also of the reality of God's mercy. To be careless or unconcerned about sin is to be careless and unconcerned about what separates us from God and others. Refusing to recognize and deal with the presence of sin in our spiritual lives is like refusing to recognize and deal with the presence of some ailment in our physical lives. Likewise, to ignore the prayer of contrition is to ignore the divine medicine that God provides to purify us of sin.

WHAT IS SIN?

Sin is a mysterious, ugly reality that can be described in countless ways.

Sin not only separates us from God and others, it also separates us from self and creation.

Sin allows our false selves to dominate our attitudes, words, and behavior.

Sin is primarily an attitude of the heart. Some people move through the day and, technically speaking, commit no sins; yet their whole attitude is sinful because they have lived their day in disregard of relationship, keeping God and people at a cool, unloving distance.

Sin is the prodigal son leaving his father's house and wanting to live his life refusing to relate with his father (see Luke 15:11-13). Cut off from his father's love, the son started to disintegrate, even to the point of eating with the swine. He had lost all self-respect. When we sin we place ourselves in a state of alienation and disintegration and in need of restoration and healing.

Sin is usually a manifestation of weakness; only rarely does it manifest malice. Most of us want to serve and love God, and we very rarely shut God out of our lives deliberately. Frequently through weakness and lack of priorities, however, we forget about God or allow other more tangible objects and people to take his place. When Peter denied that he knew Jesus, he sinned through human weakness. Frightened for his life, he became a coward and a weakling.

WHY WE
NEED CONTRITION

If sin is the cancer that destroys our peace and our relationship with God, contrition is the healing medicine that God provides to restore our peace and our relationship with him. It is faith in God's merciful love, our desire to be at peace with him, and our desire to grow in our relationship with the Lord that move us to go to God in sorrow for our sins. To the extent that we do not believe in God's mercy or desire his peace and reconciliation, to that extent we will not be very interested in praying the prayer of contrition.

"What exactly is contrition?" we may ask. Contrition is a gift that God places in our hearts to help us to see the ugliness and destructiveness of sin and to turn away from it and seek God. In his state of sin and alienation from God, the prodigal son said: "I shall get up and go to my father and I shall say to him, 'Father, I have sinned against heaven and against you. I no longer deserve to be called your son' " (Luke 15:18). So contrition is a *turning away from sin* (that which destroys life) and a *turning toward God* (the One who offers us life). Without the gift of a contrite heart we are blind to or unaware of the ugliness of sin; we have no desire to turn away from sin and return to God our Father.

HOW TO
BECOME CONTRITE

First: We should frequently pray for a contrite heart — for a heart that recognizes the destructiveness of sin, that is repentant of sin, and that once again seeks intimacy with God. Here is a suggested prayer: "Jesus, help me to see the sins (the attitudes and behaviors) in my life that block my growth in you and that hinder me from being a more loving person." Often, like King David, we are blind to the sin in our lives (see 2 Samuel 12:1-6). Also, we could use Psalm 51 (David's prayer of repentance) to pray for a contrite heart.

Second: We should pray for the grace to overcome some sinful attitude or behavior in our lives. For example, we may suffer from a critical spirit. A suggested prayer in that situation is the following: "Lord, help me to see why I tend to be so critical of others and myself. Also, Lord, grant me the grace I need to keep struggling to overcome this destructive behavior. Or better still, why don't you just rid my heart of all desire to criticize others and myself in a destructive way." Of course, we may have to pray that prayer for months or years, even a lifetime.

Third: We should pray that we feel and accept the mercy that God offers to each one of us. "Lord, help me to believe that you truly have forgiven my sins. Help me to believe that you hold no record of my past failures" (see 2 Corinthians 13:5-6). When we cannot forgive ourselves, often the problem is pride and a strong perfectionist trait in our personalities. Here we need to remember that our great need to be perfect is not a major concern for God. God knows well that if he allowed us to become perfect, we might quickly forget our need for him.

Saint Paul came to realize this when he reflected on his thorn-in-the-flesh experience. By not removing the thorn, God kept Paul in a state of humble dependence. Paul eventually saw God's wisdom and even rejoiced in it. "I will rather boast most gladly of my weaknesses, in order that the power of Christ may dwell with me'' (2 Corinthians 12:9).

Fourth: We should thank God for the gift of unceasing mercy. We can even thank God for our sins—the sins that lead us to experience his mercy, the sins that hopefully lead us to have compassion for other people in their weakness. People who think they are sinless tend to be very judgmental of others. Our sins keep us humble, dependent on God, and in need of mercy. Of course, we should always struggle to eradicate sin because sin damages our lives and destroys the harmony of God's beautiful creation (see Genesis 6:5-7).

Fifth: We should pray for true contrition. We Catholic Christians believe that sin not only diminishes our relationship with Christ but also with the members of his Body, the Church. Therefore, reconciliation of sin must include not only restoring our friendship with Christ but also with our own community of believers. In the sacrament of Penance (Reconciliation), the priest represents not only Christ but also his Body, the Church: "Whose sins you shall forgive, they are forgiven them." In the confessional, the priest is a visible, tangible sign of God's healing mercy. At this particular time and place, we hear Jesus in an audible, human way say to us, "Go in peace; your sins are forgiven." What could be more comforting, reassuring, and healing? (For more on the sacrament of Penance see the booklet, *The Sacrament of Penance: Its Past and Its Meaning for Today.* The booklet gives a brief history of the sacrament. It also explains the Rite of Penance and gives practical steps on how to make a good confession.)

REFLECTION QUESTIONS

1. What insight in these pages made the greatest impression on you?
2. "God wants to use our sins and weaknesses to bring us closer to him. The devil wants to use them to discourage us and drive us away from God." What is your reaction to this statement?
3. What sin(s) do you find it hard to forgive in others or in yourself?

4. Why, in your opinion, do some people have a difficult time forgiving themselves of some sins?
5. Do you use the prayer of contrition much? Does it work for you — that is, does it help you to restore peace with God?
6. Did you disagree with or have trouble understanding any part of this section?
7. After doing the suggested prayer exercise that follows, describe your experience.

SUGGESTED PRAYER EXERCISE

Spend some time calling to mind a past sin or failure for which you still feel unreconciled or unhealed. Then imagine Jesus being present with you. Speak with him (in word or in writing) about your failure and hurt. Then tell him you are sorry and ask him for his forgiveness and healing. Finally, imagine Jesus embracing you and restoring to you his peace and reconciliation.

6
PRAYER
OF FORGIVENESS

When you stand to pray, forgive anyone against whom you have a grievance, so that your heavenly Father may in turn forgive you your transgressions.

(Mark 11:25)

We must be reconciled with our foe lest we both perish in the vicious circle of hatred.

(Reinhold Neibuhr)

As we move through life we frequently experience hurt. We are hurt by God (when we think God doesn't answer our prayers as we would like), we are hurt by the Church and its ministers, and by other people. We hurt ourselves, and we are sometimes hurt by life. We think we are getting a raw deal. When hurt occurs, feelings of connection and warmth are replaced by feelings of alienation and coldness. We may continue to speak words to God and others, but we will not be communicating because our hearts are hurting. On the other hand, when we have the courage to give and receive forgiveness, distances are bridged, walls come tumbling down, and abysses are filled in.

Just as God wants to heal us of our sins, the Lord also wants to heal us of life's hurts. God wants to help us let go of the hurts that separate us from him and other people. But letting go of hurts is never easy. Our woundedness and pride make it difficult to give and receive forgiveness. We need God's grace to help us let go of life's hurts and accept the forgiveness that God and others offer.

Before examining some practical steps on how we can pray our way through a particular hurt, we should consider the following facts about forgiveness.

Fact One: Forgiveness doesn't mean ignoring the hurt that happened to us or putting a false label on it. Rather, it involves letting go of the hurt done to us so that the hurt is no longer a barrier to the ongoing relationship — presuming, of course, that a relationship existed prior to the hurt. Forgiveness doesn't mean trying over and over again to be friends with someone who hurts us constantly. There are some people whom we are called to love at a distance. We can do this by wishing them well and by frequently praying for them.

Fact Two: Forgiveness takes time and patience. To force our heart to be where it's not ready to be can be more of a hindrance than a help in the forgiveness process. We should not be discouraged when our first prayer efforts to forgive do not work. Forgiveness demands that we patiently bide our time.

Fact Three: Often we fail to forgive because *unconsciously* we do not want to forgive. Without realizing it, we choose to hold on to the anger and resentment we feel — perhaps because these feelings give us a sense of power over the other person.

Fact Four: Forgiveness is an act of the will and not just a matter of feelings. We can decide to forgive even though we do not feel like forgiving. Even after we have decided to forgive, we may continue to have unloving feelings for the other person. Therefore, it is important that we do not think that we have not forgiven someone just because we continue to have unloving feelings.

Fact Five: Rarely do people deliberately try to hurt us. Frequently people hurt us because they are unhappy with themselves; often people project onto others something they dislike in themselves. Their anger at others is a projection of their anger and hatred of themselves.

Fact Six: There is a difference between forgiveness and reconciliation. With the grace of God, we can always forgive a hurt, but we cannot always reconcile a hurt because it takes two people to bring about reconciliation. Jesus was able to forgive his enemies, but he was not able to be reconciled with them because they had no interest in reconciliation.

Fact Seven: Forgiveness is a gift to be prayed for over and over again. To hurt is human, but to forgive is a grace God offers to those who seek it. It is amazing how many people try to forgive and reconcile life's hurts without any recourse to God and his grace.

FOUR STEPS TO FORGIVENESS

Step One: Begin to pray amid your pain. You may begin to pray amid numerous resentful feelings and with a lack of desire to forgive. In this case you must first express in some concrete way the resentment and hurt you feel. One way to do this is to imagine the person as sitting down in front of you. Tell the person exactly how you feel. Do not mince words. Say it as it is. You may even want to punch a pillow or mattress. Also, the use of a journal to write down all your unloving and hurt feelings may be useful. Having named and expressed your feelings, then turn to Jesus and say: "Dear Jesus, right now I have no love in my heart for (name the person), and I have no desire to forgive. Please help me to let go of these negative feelings and give me a desire to forgive." You may have to pray this prayer for days or weeks before you experience any desire to forgive. It is very important that you realize that you may have to repeat a particular prayer many times.

Step Two: Repent of any wrongdoing on your part. When a rift occurs in a relationship, rarely is one party totally to blame. Yet sometimes you may see yourself as totally innocent. You adopt the stance of "righteous victim." While you may not have done anything to bring about the unloving behavior of the other person, you may not be free of resentments that have built up since the hurt occurred. There is nothing wrong with having resentful feelings — since they are neither right nor wrong — but it is wrong to allow such feelings to cause you to behave in unloving ways.

Looking at and repenting of your own contribution to the rift in the relationship is a very good thing to do. Focusing only on the other person's wrongdoing is of little help. You have no control over the other's behavior, nor are you responsible for changing it. All you can hope to do is to change yourself or your attitude toward the other person. Here your prayer might be: "Father, I confess to you the destructive and unloving ways that I have behaved in this situation. Help me to be truly sorry for my sins and fill my heart with love for (name the person)."

Step Three: Show your love by praying for the other person. This is an extremely important step in the forgiveness process. Sometimes, when dealing with a hurt, you may tend to see the other person in an exaggerated, negative way. You see him or her as really "out to get you" and "put you down." You lose sight of the woundedness (the poor self-image, fears, or "just having a bad day") that drove the other person, at least partially, to behave in such an unloving way.

One way to change all of that is simply to begin to pray for the other person. Experience shows that when you sincerely begin to pray for the well-being of another, God softens your heart and you begin to see that other person in a more loving way. As you pray, you make the other person present to you through the use of your imagination. You also imagine Jesus as being present. Ask Jesus to help you see and forgive the other as he sees and forgives everyone. Then when you are ready (which may take several prayer periods), imagine yourself beginning to smile at the person again, expressing your own forgiveness and asking the same of the other person. Follow this with an embrace.

If this use of the imagination seems a little strange, just remember how frequently you use your imaginations to "replay" the hurt. Why not use it to help heal the hurt? If you cannot forgive and embrace someone in your *imagination,* you certainly will not be able to do it in reality. Part of your prayer in this step might be to imagine Jesus as present with you and the person you want to forgive. Say: "Jesus, I know you love me and that you also love (name of other person). Please help me to see (name of person) through your eyes. Fill my hurting heart with your love for this person." As with the other suggested prayer steps, you may have to pray this step over and over again.

Step Four: Meet with the other person. This step may not take place at all — either because you have had no previous relationship with the person or because the other person is not interested in a reconciliation.

Presuming this step can and does take place, you can do a lot of praying about it. If you feel distant from a friend and yet are unaware of any hurt, you may need to pray for the strength to confront the situation and say: "I feel a coolness between us. Is there anything we need to talk about?" Pray for the courage and humility to approach the other person. Pray also for the courage to overcome the fear of rejection, and for the humility to overcome the pride that prompts you to wait for the other person to take the first step.

You should also prepare for the right timing of the meeting so that both parties may have an open and receptive attitude during the conversation. Too often people confront each other at an ill-chosen time, when one of them is very busy or tired. Pray for the right timing and the proper attitude. If you use the confrontation time just to express how wrong the other person was, you only add fuel to the fire. Avoid anything that smacks of self-righteousness or blaming the other. The attitude that has the best potential to bring about a reconciliation is the one that says: "I'm not here to point out to you how wrong you were but to say how truly sorry I am for my part in the alienation. Please forgive me." *Please forgive me* are the most healing words in the English language, and yet they are so difficult to say.

Before the meeting occurs your prayer might be something like this: "Jesus, bless the meeting I'm about to have with (name of person). Please help us to be open to your reconciling grace. Protect us from any destructive attitudes and behaviors that would block the healing process. If (name of person) is not receptive to my effort at reconciliation, still help me to express your kind of love to that person."

Obviously this step involves risk because your efforts at reconciliation may be rejected. If so, you ought to see the rejection as a genuine sharing in the Cross of Jesus, who was often rejected by the people he came to serve and redeem.

You can pray this prayer of forgiveness for people with whom you have lost contact or for people who have died. Separation or death is not a problem or an obstacle to the Spirit of God. In and through the Spirit you can forgive or ask forgiveness of a deceased person or a person with whom you have lost contact. In and through the Spirit of Jesus, who is not limited by space and time, you can make all things new. You can also use this prayer to forgive the Church or other institutions that may have hurt you. In this latter case, it might be helpful to have a conversation with some representative member of the institution. For example, where the conflict has been with the Church, a conversation with a priest or minister might facilitate the healing process and give it some flesh.

In conclusion, it helps to realize that this whole area of forgiveness and reconciliation is as varied and as complex as there are people who experience conflict and hurt. You must be careful, therefore, not to generalize or universalize one or two particular experiences. The author himself knows from the positive responses that he has received from his book, *How to Forgive Yourself and Others: Steps to Reconciliation,* that prayer suggestions like these have helped countless numbers of people let go of hurts and reconcile interpersonal conflicts.

REFLECTION QUESTIONS

1. What insight in these pages made the greatest impression on you?
2. Often you will fail in your efforts to forgive because *unconsciously* you do not want to forgive. What is your reaction to that statement?
3. How do you normally forgive and reconcile a hurt?
4. Did you disagree with or have trouble understanding any part of this section?
5. After doing the suggested prayer exercise that follows, describe your experience.

SUGGESTED PRAYER EXERCISE

Identify a hurt or grievance that you cling to and that you haven't let go of yet. Then pray about it for a period of time, using the four steps offered in this chapter.

7
PRAYER
OF CONSCIOUSNESS
EXAMEN

Mary kept all these things, reflecting on them in her heart.

(Luke 2:19)

To some extent, each of us tends to live in a state of wakeful sleep, more or less consciously going through the motions of our every-day life and experience. Rarely do we take time to get in touch with and to reflect upon the deeper meanings of our experiences. We tend to think that such reflection is simply a waste of time.

(Claire Brissette)

The key challenge of the spiritual life is to lead a life that is in tune with the Holy Spirit so that we can be guided along the path that God created for us. Saint John says, ''Whoever has ears ought to hear what the Spirit says to the churches'' (Revelation 2:7). Insofar as we do not have sensitive spiritual ears to hear the words of the Spirit, we run the risk of traveling in all directions, led not by the Holy Spirit but by inner, uncontrolled impulses and outer, passing fads. Like Martha we may become busy doing many good things but missing out on what the Lord is telling us (see Luke 10:38-42). Or, like the Israelites, we may spend many years traveling a part of the spiritual journey that we could have traveled in a much shorter time if we had learned to listen and respond to the promptings of the Holy Spirit. We can say that a key aspect of spiritual growth is learning to become a *spirit-listener.*

One of the best spiritual exercises we have available to help us to become spirit-listeners is the Consciousness Examen. The Con-sciousness Examen is a spiritual exercise popularized by Saint

Ignatius of Loyola. Jesuit Father George Aschenbrenner, with an article entitled "Consciousness Examen" in the *Review for Religious,* has helped us rediscover this reflective exercise. It is said that Saint Ignatius used to tell his novices that if they had to omit all the spiritual exercises of the day but one, he would want them to be faithful to the Consciousness Examen.

The main purpose of this spiritual exercise is not to tally up the failures or successes of the day, as we often do in the traditional examination of conscience, but to help us to grow in our sensitivity and responsiveness to the voice of the Holy Spirit. The exercise helps us to see how attentive and responsive we were to the Holy Spirit in the encounters and events of a given day. It also helps us to become conscious of how our sinful side may be luring us away from the Father's loving call and leading us to live a life according to the flesh. Lastly, it helps us to integrate prayer and the activities of our day.

While some writers identify five steps in the Consciousness Examen, this exercise will be divided into three steps, with the third step including the other two steps.

THREE STEPS
IN THE EXAMEN PROCESS

Step One: Pray to the Holy Spirit for guidance and courage. We begin by taking a minute or two to quiet down and become aware of God's loving presence. We know in faith — even if we can't feel it — that God loves us unconditionally. When we know we are loved in this manner, we usually find it easier to look at the less attractive sides of our personality. This demands courage on our part. This is why it is important to ask the Holy Spirit to help us face our true selves. Having relaxed and entered into the presence of God, we then pray to the Holy Spirit for guidance and courage.

The following prayer is most appropriate: "Holy Spirit, help me to see the encounters and events of this day as you would want me to see them. Since I cannot focus on or look at everything, help me to reflect on the encounters or events that you would want me to consider. Also give me the courage to face my inner demons, the attitudes and behaviors on which I'd prefer not to reflect."

Step Two: As led by the Spirit, reflect on a particular event or encounter. Having prayed to the Spirit, we should take a minute or two to allow the events and encounters of the day to come before our mental television screen and decide on an event or encounter on which to focus. When we decide on a particular event or encounter, we should try to see and be in touch with what was happening in that event. What were our attitudes and behavior like? Were we being true to ourselves or acting like frauds? Here we may look back and see that God was inviting us to listen to someone but we decided to turn that person off and center on our own preoccupations. Perhaps we felt the Spirit prompting us to offer a word of encouragement or affirmation, to seek forgiveness, but we decided to be silent and distant.

Another way to look at the day is to ask:

- ''To what extent was my day Christ-centered, other-centered, or self-centered?''
- ''When I got up in the morning and moved through the day, what attitudes or behaviors dominated? Was I loving, caring, aggressive, or short-tempered?''
- ''Did I try to meet people and events in a Christlike way, or was I basically concerned only about myself and my projects?''
- ''To what extent did I reverence Christ in the people I met? Did I treat people in a utilitarian way, basing my response to them on the basis of their usefulness to me and my projects?''

Such reflection should help us grow in self-knowledge and help us to be more aware of the attitudes and behaviors that dominate the flow of our days.

Step Three: Offer prayers of thanks, repentance, healing, and petition. Having reflected on some event(s) or encounter(s) of the day, we can now spend a few minutes talking to the Lord about our good and not-so-good responses. It is such a conversation that changes what might be a self-centered, introspective reflection into a God-centered one.

For the blessings of the day we give thanks. Also we should give thanks for the times we manifested caring attitudes and behaviors, for the times we recognized the Spirit's promptings and responded positively.

For the negative and unloving attitudes and behaviors, for the times we did not respond as the Lord was asking us to respond, we seek God's forgiveness. For negative attitudes and behaviors that reveal not so much our sinfulness but our woundedness and tiredness, we ask for God's healing and strength.

For the help, strength, and courage we need to continue our desire to hear God's voice and our efforts to do his will in all things, we can offer prayers of petition. Also we can ask God's blessing on the people we met that day, especially those who were hurting and whom we may have hurt in some way.

Ideally, we should set aside a quiet time each evening for the Consciousness Examen, but we may often have to settle for less than the ideal. Therefore, we may find ourselves doing this spiritual exercise on our way home from work, when jogging, when in the shower, as a family at dinner, or as we lie down to sleep at night.

What is important here is not so much when and how we make a Consciousness Examen but that we actually take time for this prayer activity. Without regular periods of reflective silence in the presence of God, we will fail to grow in self-knowledge; we will be out of touch with our feelings and inner urgings; and, worst of all, we will become people who are driven and controlled by our excessive needs, desires, compulsions, and inordinate attachments. The noisy crowd and not the noiseless Spirit will become our guide. (An excellent resource on helping us to live life more reflectively is Claire Brissette's *Reflective Living: A Spiritual Approach to Everyday Living.*)

REFLECTION QUESTIONS

1. What insight in these pages made the greatest impression on you?
2. "Insofar as we do not develop an inner spiritual ear, we will run the risk of traveling in all kinds of directions, not led by the Spirit of God but by inner, uncontrolled impulses and outer, passing fads." What is your reaction to this statement?
3. Can you see a difference in the way you respond to life when you live reflectively and when you live unreflectively?

4. What is the thing that helps you most of all to keep your focus on the Lord?
5. Did you disagree with or have trouble understanding any part of this section?
6. After doing the suggested prayer exercise that follows, describe your experience.

SUGGESTED PRAYER EXERCISE

Several times this week, take ten minutes (preferably toward the end of the day) to pray reflectively in the manner outlined in this chapter.

8
PRAYING WITH
A SPIRITUAL JOURNAL

Take a scroll and write on it all the words I have spoken to you.
(Jeremiah 36:2)

Journal keeping clearly . . . has a past and present tradition in the
Church as a valued way of growing in the likeness of Christ and a
helpful method of praying.

(Joseph M. Champlin)

Journals serve different purposes for different people. Some
people keep them just to log the events of daily life. For others,
journal-keeping can be a form of therapy. Saint Augustine used
writing to unburden his conscience. Emerson said that no matter
how disheveled the day, all disasters seem less painful in the
evening once they are recorded. When Dag Hammarskjold began
keeping a journal he called it "a sort of white book concerning my
negotiations with myself and with God."

Journaling helps us to place the days and years of our lives in
proper perspective. Judged by the days — each one viewed
individually — life does not make sense. Judged by the years,
however, it does add up and a plan emerges. Professor Ed Fischer
(in an article appearing in the *Notre Dame Magazine*) writes:

A good reason to write a memoir is to have the satisfaction, the
consolation of seeing a pattern form. . . . A journal can help you
find a pattern in your life, a theme, a recurring motif. . . . It will
help you get a glimpse of what you are becoming. Rereading a
journal is like coming upon a wall where in youth you stood from
time to time to chalk your height, or like paging through an old
family album. How you changed and you didn't even notice!

The reflections of Professor Fischer should help us to see how journal-keeping in general can serve many useful and wonderful purposes. The purpose of a *spiritual* journal, however, is more specific and focused. Its primary aim is to help us live our lives more in tune with the Spirit of God, to help us detect the thread of God's weaving in our daily lives. In a spiritual journal we try to identify the leadings of the Spirit in our lives and record how we are responding or not responding to such leadings. We search for what helps or hinders us from hearing and responding to the Spirit in our daily events and encounters. As we discipline ourselves to write in our journals and reread our entries periodically, we will be able to detect trends and patterns — where we are coming from and where we are going in life.

A spiritual journal is an excellent tool to help us slow down in a fast-moving world and develop a reflective attitude toward life. It is a way to identify and record the moods, voices, fantasies, daydreams, anxieties and blessings of a given day — a way to name, vent, and defuse the tough feelings of life and try to see all these in terms of our relationship with God. Using a spiritual journal gives us a chance to meet the Lord in a new way, to personalize our faith, and to learn the difference between our stated and lived values. If we work with a spiritual director, a spiritual journal can help us to remember what has been going on in our life since our previous meeting.

Some people use a spiritual journal to write "letters to God." Father Henri Nouwen's book, *A Cry for Mercy: Prayers From the Genesee,* is an excellent example of such letter writing to God. This book gives an inside view of the spiritual life of one of the world's most popular writers and speakers. In this book he offers a "soul-teaching" on prayer.

IMPORTANCE OF HONESTY

Honesty is a very important part of journal-keeping. What probably inhibits our honesty most is the fear of someone reading what we have written down. Consequently, we tend to write only what we want "posterity" to know about us. We should, of course, do all that we can to resist the temptations of the false self that tells us to write only the nice things.

To help protect the privacy of my journal, I always write on the inside cover, "Private Journal: Please Do Not Read." Then, I conceal personal names by using initials or even by creating nicknames. Some kind of shorthand or code-word system could also be used, and the journal could be kept under lock and key. For me the fear of someone reading my journal has diminished. I have been greatly helped in letting go of this fear by my belief that what is most personally and intimately felt is also most universally felt. If people are scandalized by my wilder thoughts, fantasies, and feelings, it is only because they are out of touch with the evil or shadowy side of their own personalities.

FOUR SUGGESTIONS
FOR JOURNAL WRITING

What is a good way to keep a journal? In answer to that question, here are some suggestions that should prove helpful.

First suggestion: Come to a place of quiet. (This could even be a bench in the center of a shopping mall or a seat on an airplane or train.) Anyway, begin by quieting down within. We can then become aware of God's love and ask his Spirit to help us become aware of what is going on within us right now or during the past few hours or days.

Then we can ask: "What do I find myself daydreaming about? What thoughts are on my mind when I wake up in the middle of the night or in the morning? What are my pressing concerns right now?" As we become aware of what is going on within us, we can begin to jot it down. It is very important to avoid at this point any moralizing on what is flowing out from within. We should put all judgment aside, at least temporarily, and simply allow ourselves to freely express our spontaneous thoughts and feelings. There is no need to analyze or dissect our experiences. Just "be there" with them and see what they might be telling us about our inner self.

In order to do this we will often have to tell our inner voices (like our ideal self or intellectual self) to be quiet. As we write, or after we have finished, we should invite Jesus to be a part of the process. We can tell him how we feel about what we have written. Then we should pause and try to become aware of what we think Jesus would say to us in response. This may be difficult initially or seem to be contrived. But the fact is that the Spirit of Jesus lives within us and we can assume that he would want to say something to us about the stuff going on in our lives. It would be very good to share with a spiritual director the words we place in Jesus' mouth because these words would very much reflect our image of God, which may or may not be very distorted.

Second suggestion: Use the journal to get in touch with a troublesome mood that may be "possessing" us at any given moment of the day. Until such a mood or "demon" is named and rebuked, it will have power over us and be an obstacle to our efforts to live our day in a Christlike manner. (For a good testament on bad moods and the spiritual life, consult Chapter Three of *Moving in the Spirit,* by Richard Hauser, S.J.)

Third suggestion: Use the journal to express and deal with tough feelings which may have arisen because of some issue or encounter. It is good to journal about an anxiety or insecurity we are feeling within ourself or about angry or jealous feelings. When the feelings we have within are related to some relationship or some encounter we had with another person, we may find it useful to imagine that person sitting down in front of us.

At this point I personally use the journal to "speak my mind" and say my bit, grateful that I cannot be interrupted or do not have to be worried about what I say. Martin Luther found that to rage against his enemies helped him to pray better. A journal is a good place to rage. If the released rage leaves more space in the heart for prayer, that alone is a good reason for keeping a journal.

In both of the above situations (dealing with troublesome moods or with tough feelings) we should invite Jesus to be a part of what is going on. We could say, "Jesus, this is what is going on with me; please help me with it." Then we should pause and become one with our moods as we give them to Jesus. We can imagine him looking at us with eyes of love and concern. Then we can invite his response with the words, "Speak, Lord, your servant is listening." Often we may be afraid to face what is within us and be scared to bring it to Jesus, unsure of how he may react. But if we can't face and befriend the "enemy" within, how can we expect to face and befriend the enemies outside of us?

Fourth suggestion: Use the spiritual journal to identify some helps and hindrances in our lives as we try to live in the Spirit or as we attempt to become more flexible clay in the hands of our Divine Lord whose great plan is to reshape us in the image and likeness of Jesus.

These four suggestions should help those who wish to use a spiritual journal as part of their prayer life. People who feel drawn to this way of praying — spiritual journaling is not for everyone — could search out other resources that give many practical suggestions on how to make the spiritual journal a valuable means of spiritual growth. There are numerous books that treat the subject of spiritual journaling, but the one entitled *Challenge,* by Jesuit Mark Link, is outstanding because it is based on the Spiritual Exercises of Saint Ignatius and offers readers ninety-one meditations and questions for journaling purposes. The bibliography lists several other good books on this topic.

REFLECTION QUESTIONS

1. What insight in these pages made the greatest impression on you?
2. Have you had any experience with a spiritual journal? If so, what has been your reaction?
3. In what ways do you think spiritual journaling could aid you in your prayer life?
4. Did you disagree with or have trouble understanding any part of this section?
5. After doing the suggested prayer exercise that follows, describe your experience.

SUGGESTED PRAYER EXERCISE

Take ten to fifteen minutes to journal about your own death. Ask yourself: What would you find most difficult about dying? What would you fear most? What would you want to say to your friends before you die? What would you want to be remembered for? What words would you want on your tombstone?

9
DECISIONING PRAYER

Choose life, then, that you and your descendants may live, by loving the LORD, your God, heeding his voice, and holding fast to him. For that will mean life for you.

(Deuteronomy 30:19-20)

Since the mysterious voice of the Spirit is not the only voice we hear but comes to us accompanied by the tumultuous sounds of our own conflicting impulses and the clamoring of the entire creation, it is essential for us to be able to discern the presence of the Spirit in order to choose to say "yes" to him.

(Thomas Green, S.J.)

"Should I marry John?"

"Should I get out of or stay in this unhappy marriage?"

"Should I quit my present career and take up something less lucrative but more fulfilling?"

"Should I join or quit a particular ministry in my parish or community?"

Decisions, decisions, decisions. . . . Life is full of them, big and small, and sometimes it seems so difficult to know exactly what God is asking of us. When it comes to decision-making, many of us would like very much to dial Heaven 27 and say, as I do: "Hi, Lord, this is your friend Eamon. I am faced with this particular decision, and I was wondering which way I ought to go. Could you please let me know as soon as possible. Thanks."

Even though no such direct line to God exists, that is not to say that no divine guidance is available to us. As Christians we believe that because the Holy Spirit lives in our hearts (see 1 Corinthians 6:19) we can indeed come to a good sense of his truth for our lives.

Before he left this world to return to his Father, Jesus promised us the gift of his Spirit. He told his disciples, "I will ask the Father, and he will give you another Advocate to be with you always, the Spirit of truth" (John 14:16-17). A central activity of the Holy Spirit in our lives is to lead us into the truth by helping us to discover and walk God's path for our lives. Because the Holy Spirit is not the only voice that seeks to guide us in life, we Christians need help when it comes to decision-making. Besides the voice of God, there are many other voices that call out to us, seeking to attract us and influence us to walk in a particular direction.

Even a quick reading of modern-day literature on Christian decision-making (often called discernment) helps us to see that the decision-making process can be a rather complex process, basically due to our lack of self-knowledge, our lack of inner freedom, and our great ability to try to have God say "yes" to what we ourselves want. Yet none of this should discourage us. With the Holy Spirit on our side and with a willingness to learn — through reading, through dialoguing with other mature Christians, and especially through the trial-and-error method — we will be pleasantly surprised at how quickly we can grow in our ability to recognize and discern the voice of God from voices that are not of the Lord. One of the best spiritual exercises available to help us to grow in the art of Christian decision-making is the Prayer of Consciousness Examen outlined in Chapter Seven.

Do we have available any practical ways to help us discover God's will in a specific situation? There are no foolproof ways that will lead us to absolute certainty concerning God's will in a particular situation, but there are specific guidelines that can help us to grow in our ability to perceive and discern God's call and action in our lives. These steps could be called: *A Beginner's Guide to Christian Decision-Making*. As we grow in the art and gift of discernment or decision-making, we will develop a method that best works for us.

I will give here only a summary of the steps that are dealt with in greater detail in my booklet, *Help for Making Difficult Decisions*. This 32-page booklet also explores some specifics that help and hinder individuals at decision-making time.

Here are seven steps that should help bring our prayer life into our decision-making process.

SEVEN STEPS
TO DISCERNMENT

First Step: Formulate a proposition. We start by making a clear statement or question of what we are trying to decide. For example: "Should I change careers?" "Should I terminate my relationship with so-and-so?" "Should I join a particular ministry in my parish?"

Second Step: Gather the relevant data. Write down the various alternatives available and consider the advantages and disadvantages of each. We need to take into consideration the effect each alternative would have on our relationship with God, our family, or any other individual(s) or group(s). As we end this step, we need to identify the alternative or option that we feel most drawn toward or the option to which we feel most attached.

Third Step: Bring the gathered data to prayer. This is the heart of the discernment process. It involves praying about the available options before the Lord with the purpose of seeing which option gives us the greatest sense of God's peace. As we pray, it is important for us to see if there is one option that we feel we want more than the others. If there is, then we need to ask: "How willing am I to let go of that option if it seems God is calling me in another direction?" In other words, how free and willing are we to embrace any option that the Lord might offer? Often we are so attached to a particular direction that we are not free to move in another direction — hence, the vital importance of praying for the grace of inner freedom.

We are at the point of *inner freedom* when we are detached enough from every available option to be free to walk down any path that the Lord may call us to walk. Sometimes it may take weeks or even months to come to that point of detachment or inner freedom. Ideally, we should not choose a *particular* option until we are free to embrace every available option. We need to be aware that where there exists a strong attachment to a particular option, the discernment process is endangered and our capacity for recognizing God's call is blurred. Of course, in some situations we may never reach the state of complete detachment. That's okay and understandable, but at least we must have a desire for complete detachment and struggle toward that goal.

Personally I find this part of the discernment process to be the most important and the most challenging. It is not easy to say in all sincerity: "Thy Kingdom come, not mine. Thy will be done, not mine." Of course, with God's grace all things are possible.

As we engage in the struggle to embrace God's will, it is important for us to know that our deepest and truest self desires God's will. It is our false, sinful, and unredeemed self that resists God's will. But it is God's will which leads us to true freedom and true happiness. The voice in us that does not believe this is the voice of the false self, not the true self.

As we pray about the various options available, we need to distinguish between what we think and feel when we are in prayer and most open to God's will and what we think and feel outside of prayer when we might be anxious and attached to a particular option. The former is more likely to be God's will for us.

As a part of this third step, Saint Ignatius suggests three imaginative exercises. *First,* we should consider what advice we would give to another person faced with the same situation. *Second,* we can imagine ourselves on our deathbed and ask what we would then wish to have chosen. *Third,* we can picture ourselves standing before God on the Last Day and consider what decision we would then wish to have made. These exercises help us to distance ourselves from the decision facing us and to look at it with some objectivity.

Fourth Step: Make a decision. At some point we must make a decision. We should go with the option that gives us the most peace when we are in prayer. But what if we experience no real peace about the options available to us? In that situation, we can either postpone the decision or choose the one least troublesome to us. We should not decide when in doubt; and, if time permits, we should continue to pray until we experience peace about a particular option. Last, we need to be aware that the option chosen may not always be the most attractive one or the one we most desired. Sometimes we may feel led to choose an option with tears — for example, to return to a marriage situation that in the past caused much pain. However, such initial tears of sadness often give way to tears of joy (see 2 Corinthians 7:8-13).

Fifth Step: Live with the decision. Once we come to a decision, it is good to live with it for a while before we actually act on what we decided. This is particularly important if we have a tendency to be impulsive.

Sixth Step: Act on the decision. This may seem obvious, but this step can be the most difficult because it may involve giving up something to which we are still quite attached. We should ask the Holy Spirit to give us the power and courage to act on what we believe to be God's will for our lives.

Seventh Step: Seek confirmation of the decision. Father Matthew Linn reminds us that the final test for hearing God's will is whether living it out brings life to us and to others. If the choice we make bears good fruit, we can be quite sure we acted in accord with God's will. This is not to say that there won't be struggles connected with our choice nor days when we will wonder, "Did I really make the right choice?" Such struggles and wondering are normal and do not necessarily prove that we made a wrong decision.

Now what if we discover later that we did make the wrong decision? Knowing that we made a sincere effort to seek God's will should console us. Discernment is not just a gift but an art learned through trial and error. The Lord doesn't ask that we always be right; God asks only that we always try to be honest and act out of our best understanding of a particular situation. Finally, we can be consoled by remembering God's ability to use our mistakes to his — and our — advantage. God writes straight with crooked lines.

To prepare our hearts for good decision-making, the following prayer by Saint Ignatius of Loyola is recommended:

> Take, Lord, and receive
> all my liberty,
>> my memory,
>> my understanding,
>> and my will,
>> all that I have and possess.
>> Everything I have is yours,
>> for you have given it all to me;
>> to you I return it.

Take, Lord, and do what you
like with me,
only give me your grace
and your love,
for that is enough for me.
                              Amen.

REFLECTION QUESTIONS

1. What insight in these pages made the greatest impression on you?
2. Recall a difficult decision you have had to make. Explain why it was difficult and how you finally reached the decision you did.
3. How do you usually make decisions? Do you follow your head or your heart? Do you write down the pros and cons of the options available? Do you seek the counsel of others?
4. Can you think of a particular decision you made which was wrong but which God turned to his — and your — advantage?
5. Did you disagree with or have trouble understanding any part of this section?
6. After doing the suggested prayer exercise that follows, describe your experience.

SUGGESTED PRAYER EXERCISE

Write down decisions facing you at this time in your life and begin to ask the Holy Spirit to guide you in making them. If the decision needed is an immediate one, use the practical steps offered in this chapter and see how they help you.

10
PRAYER OF REFLECTIVE
SPIRITUAL READING

All scripture is inspired of God and is useful for teaching, for refutation, for correction, and for training in righteousness.

(2 Timothy 3:16)

It is a good thing to have a spiritual book to feed your prayer. What sort of book? It must be a book which "clicks" with you personally, a book you feel at home with like a wise and trusted friend, a book which speaks to your condition. People are always recommending books to us. "You must read so and so; you must read such and such." By all means have a look at them, have a quick browse through, but unless the recommended book "clicks" with you, forget it. It is not the book for you now. It may be one day, but not now. We are all made differently, we all have different needs and we are all at different stages on the road. Choose your own book and read it slowly, a little at a time, pausing to think about it, to chew it over, to take it in.

(Evan Pilkington)

The Church has always considered reflective or spiritual reading to be one of the most fundamental exercises of the spiritual life. In and through this meditative type of reading, especially on the gospels, we come to know the person of Christ and the attitudes and values he embraces. Spiritual reading also nourishes, illumines, and gives direction to our deepest selves, our spirits. Without regular periods of reflective reading, we run the risk of becoming victims of passing fads and of allowing ourselves to be led by the wisdom of the world — that wisdom which is contrary to the wisdom of the gospels and the spiritual masters.

If we decide to use a sacred text as part of our prayer time, we must realize that reflective spiritual reading differs greatly from the reading of a textbook, a novel, or a newspaper. In fact, if we approach spiritual reading the way we approach the reading of a textbook or novel, we run the risk of creating unnecessary obstacles to God's revelation and touch.

DIFFERENCE BETWEEN INFORMATIVE AND FORMATIVE READING

Reflective reading is called *formative* and the other types of reading are called *informative,* according to the teachings of Father Adrian van Kaam, founder of the School of Formative Spirituality at Duquesne University, and Dr. Susan Muto, the school's Executive Director.

Informative reading makes use of our intellect or what is sometimes called our "computer intelligence." We read by gathering information or data, analyzing it, comparing it, and categorizing it into neat sections. We usually use the informative approach to scan the newspaper, prepare facts for a meeting, cram for an exam, or master some material we have to teach. This approach is basically utilitarian in nature. Our aim is to gather and manage information that may be useful to us in our daily life. During this process we are in charge. We keep studying a certain text or book until we master it. This type of reading nourishes and satisfies the hunger of the mind to know and to understand things. Most of us have been trained to read or study in this way. Needless to say, the informative approach to reading and to life serves many useful purposes. It enables us to achieve much and to bring some kind of order into the chaos of our lives.

In contrast to the informative approach to reading, the reflective or formative approach demands a different mind-set and a whole new set of attitudes. With this approach, we move into the slow lane of life. There is no reason to feel that we have to get through a certain amount of chapters or pages in one session. On the contrary, we may spend thirty minutes on a few lines of a text. The phrases that are most frequently used to describe the formative approach are: *gentle dwelling, patient abiding, respectful listen-*

ing, humble openness, and receptivity. We read and gently dwell on the words and phrases of a text. Then we wait with humble openness and receptivity for the Holy Spirit to reveal its hidden treasures. For example, in reflecting on Psalm 23, listen to the Lord say: "I am *your* Shepherd . . . *you* shall not want, . . . " and so on.

As mature reflective or formative readers, we are well aware that it is not our cleverness but the power of the Holy Spirit that enables us to receive spiritual food and direction from a given text. We are not in control. Instead we are humble disciples waiting in humble openness for the Master to break open the treasures of a particular text. When we engage in this type of reading, we should always pray to the Holy Spirit for sensitive, spiritual ears to hear the words of the Master. The principle aim is not to analyze, dissect, or gather information out of a sacred passage. The goal of reflective reading is to facilitate spiritual transformation and to allow the sacred words to penetrate our deepest selves for the purpose of spiritual nourishment, illumination, and direction for our lives. Our purpose is to make connections between the text we read and our present life in all its diversity.

We can quickly see that there is quite a difference between the informative and formative approaches to reading. We can also see that if most of the reading we do is of the informative nature, it will not be easy for us to change gears and move into the slow lane of formative reading. We need to remember that spiritual reading is an art to be learned. It involves, among other things, learning to be sensitive to the stirrings of the Spirit as we read, having the discipline to respond to those stirrings, and saying "No" to the compulsion of our informative side to read quickly and cover as much territory as possible.

SEVEN STAGES
OF FORMATIVE READING

Our primary sources of spiritual or sacred reading are Holy Scripture, the spiritual classics, and good contemporary spiritual books. Any of these texts can be a meeting place for us and the Lord where God can speak, illumine, and nourish our deepest selves.

Now that we have examined the characteristics of formative reading, it is imperative that we learn how to read in this way. There are seven stages in the process:

Stage One: Moving in the slow lane and entering the presence of God. Ideally, we should engage in formative reading when our minds are fresh and rested. If we come to sacred reading in a state of overstimulation — with ideas, plans, concerns, anxieties — our minds and hearts will find it difficult, if not impossible, to be receptive. There is so much happening inside us that the "Word" cannot "happen." If we do find ourselves a little tense as we are about to begin a time of formative reading, we can usually help ourselves to relax by taking a few deep breaths and by becoming aware of the presence of God within us. As we begin to relax we should also try to become aware of and present to all that is going on within us — our thoughts, feelings, agitations, whatever. If we are experiencing some tough feelings like anger, apprehension, loneliness, or hurt, we should bring these feelings before Jesus, remembering that he had similar feelings. "In the days when he [Jesus] was in the flesh, he offered prayers and supplications with loud cries and tears to the one who was able to save him from death" (Hebrews 5:7).

Stage Two: Seeking the help of the Holy Spirit. Before he returned to his Father, Jesus said, "The Advocate, the holy Spirit that the Father will send in my name — he will teach you everything and remind you of all that [I] told you" (John 14:26). In his Last Supper discourse, Jesus also said, "Without me you can do nothing" (John 15:5). So, before we begin to reflect on a sacred text (especially a Scripture passage), we need to take a moment to ask the Holy Spirit to guide and inspire our reading, to reveal to us the hidden treasures of this text, and to be open to whatever challenge the sacred words may issue to us. Sometimes our main problem in reading the Scriptures is not that we lack a good method. Our problem is that we do not have the love, the courage, and the generosity to allow God's Word to take possession of our hearts and change our lives.

The next four stages of this process employ the image of a ladder focusing on the four rungs by which we are lifted up to heaven. This "ladder" image is based on the story in Genesis 28:10-22 where Jacob sees a ladder reaching to the heavens. The names of the four rungs of this ladder are:

- *Lectio:* Reading of the Word.
- *Meditatio:* Meditation on the Word.
- *Oratio:* Praying or responding to the Word that we have read and upon which we have meditated.
- *Contemplatio:* Contemplating or resting in wordless communion with the Word.

Stage Three: *Lectio* — Slowly and prayerfully allowing the word to enter us. During the *lectio* (reading) stage of our spiritual reading exercise, our aim is simply to be attentive to the words of the chosen text. We are not yet reflecting on them. Our aim is to just allow the words to enter our being — to allow them to soak into our hearts as a gentle rain soaks into the earth. We can continue to read (and reread) slowly the words of the text until some word or phrase grabs hold of us. When this happens we should pause and proceed to the next rung of the ladder—namely, *meditatio.*

Stage Four: *Meditatio* — Gently dwelling on and reacting to the Word. As we read a text and a word speaks to us as never before, we are experiencing the gift of the Holy Spirit breaking open for us the meaning of the word. When this happens we should pause and become present to this "word of salvation," as it is sometimes called. Then we can react to the phrase, sentence, or verse that gripped us. If *lectio* is reading or receiving the Word, *meditatio* is reacting to the Word. Suppose our chosen text was the well-known Emmaus story (see Luke 24:13-35) and the verse that struck us was, "Their eyes were prevented from recognizing him." Our *meditatio* or reflection on those words might be: "The two disciples were so absorbed in their own problems that they were unable to recognize the one who joined them. But Jesus was patient. He didn't push the disciples to recognize him. He just walked with them, sensitive to their anguish, waiting patiently for their eyes to be opened." Then we can start to ponder how often in life's journey our eyes are restrained from recognizing Jesus in our midst through an encounter or event in the course of the day. We can become aware of some attitudes in our life, like preoccupation with self, that block us from seeing Jesus.

Our reaction to a different text may be one of confusion; like the disciples, we might wonder, "What can these words mean?" — anger ("How could Jesus say such a thing?"), joy and consolation, or resistance (when the text challenges our lifestyle and values). When we are finished reacting or reflecting on a text, we are now ready to move to the next rung of the ladder — namely, *oratio*.

Stage Five: *Oratio* — Responding to the Word spoken to us. *Oratio* is our response to the Word that the Lord has spoken to us. A passage, verse, or sentence from Scripture or some other spiritual book may have consoled us, inspired us, challenged us, convicted us, or called us to repentance. Now is the time to respond to the Lord about the Word he has given us and upon which we have meditated. The important point here is to be honest when we answer. Our response to the verse in the Emmaus story (see Luke 24:16) might be: "Lord, I become so preoccupied with myself and my concerns that I am often blind to your presence as I walk the journey of life. Please open my eyes to your presence in the people and events of today. Thank you, Lord, for being willing to walk with me in the Emmaus journeys of my life."

To different texts our prayer might be: "Lord, I am scared of what you ask of me in this text. I am not ready to give up everything and follow you," and so forth. In times of spiritual dryness, our response might be: "Lord, this Word says nothing to me. I feel so empty. Lord, I find it hard to cope with such emptiness and dryness. I'm afraid that I am losing you. I wonder why you do not come to me. Lord, have mercy and help me to be patient." Such a response will please God very much because it is honest and from the heart.

Stage Six: *Contemplatio* — Resting with the Word. Contemplation is regarded as the highest form of prayer. It is present when we stop reading *(lectio)*, thinking *(meditatio)*, speaking *(oratio)*, and begin resting silently in the Lord's presence. It is like the experience of two friends enjoying each other's presence without speaking. They may turn to each other in an embrace of wordless communication. In contemplation we are aware that we are in God and he is in us, and that is all we need right now. After our period of *contemplatio,* if time permits, we may begin the process all over again. We begin to read again (Stage Three) until some word strikes us. Then we pause and reflect on it, repeating the entire process.

Stage Seven: Concluding with a prayer of thanksgiving. We should end our formative reading time with a prayer of thanksgiving. We can give thanks to the Lord for any insights received or for the experience of his loving presence. We should give thanks even if we think we received nothing and are being sent away empty. We may well have received many spiritual gifts, especially the great gift of learning to love and remain faithful to prayer in spite of a lack of any tangible sign of God's presence and activity.

Now, here are two points to keep in mind when we use this type of prayer.

First: If we keep a spiritual journal, we may want to keep a log of the texts, the "words of salvation," that we receive from the Lord in formative reading. These "words of salvation" can be read over and over and allowed to nourish, illumine, and give direction to our deepest self.

Second: If while reflecting on a certain text — for example, the one about turning the other cheek — we find ourselves struggling with the message, we should stay with it and try to become aware of the reasons why we are resisting it. "Is the text asking too much of us?" "Is it questioning some attitude or behavior that we don't want to let go of?" "Do we simply have a hard time believing the truth of the text?"

We should also try to talk to the Lord about the text, telling him of our problems with it. We may initially feel ashamed or embarrassed at our resistance, finding it difficult to talk openly to the Lord. At such times we should remember that Jesus, who struggled in Gethsemane with what his Father was asking of him, will most surely understand our struggles and resistances. This is where honesty in prayer is vital. There is always the temptation to avoid talking about hard and unpleasant matters in our lives. But if our relationship with God (and other people) is going to be real, we must do all that we can to lay all our cards on the table.

The format described here is only one way to do formative reading; there are many other variations. Readers are urged to use the parts of this format that help them to make the sacred text a meeting place for the reader and the Lord. Whatever facilitates that meeting is a good method. Whatever hinders that meeting is a bad method.

REFLECTION QUESTIONS

1. What insight in these pages made the greatest impression on you?
2. What format do you usually use when reading a sacred text? Could your method be enriched in any way by the seven-stage method treated in this chapter?
3. Besides the Bible, what spiritually enriching books have you read recently and why were they so enriching?
4. When reading or listening to the Word of God in the Bible, do you ever experience ''resistance'' to certain texts? If so, how do you usually handle the situation?
5. Did you disagree with or have trouble understanding any part of this section?
6. After doing the suggested prayer exercise that follows, describe your experience.

SUGGESTED PRAYER EXERCISE

Take a passage of Scripture or a passage from a nonscriptural spiritual book and reflect on it, using the format described in this chapter. When you are finished, spend a few minutes identifying what you liked and did not like about the format.

11
PRAYER
OF CONTEMPLATION

All of us, gazing with unveiled face on the glory of the Lord, are being transformed into the same image from glory to glory, as from the Lord who is the Spirit.

(2 Corinthians 3:18)

All those who engage in this work of contemplation find that it has a good effect on the body as well as on the soul, for it makes them attractive in the eyes of all who see them. So much so that the ugliest person alive who becomes, by grace, a contemplative finds that he suddenly (and again by grace) is different, and that every good man he sees is glad and happy to have his friendship, and is spiritually refreshed, and helped nearer God by his company.

(The Cloud of Unknowing)

The majority of Christians do not think that contemplative prayer is for "ordinary Christians." Most people would tend to say, "That's only for monks and religious who live in monasteries." Perhaps the reason why many of us think that way is because we have preconceived concepts of contemplative prayer as something very lofty, mystical, and far beyond the capacity of the ordinary Christian. On the contrary, contemplative prayer is possible for anyone who is interested in becoming *more aware* of the realities encountered in everyday life. It is possible for anyone who is willing to stop *being constantly on the go* to *be still* in contemplative prayer before the God who is the Ground of all being. Furthermore, contemplative prayer is something that most of us have experienced or done without actually calling it by that name.

William Shannon, President of the International Thomas Merton Society, describes contemplation in this way: "Contemplation is being in the presence of God and letting go of thoughts, images, desires, concerns, anxieties. I let go of all that is not God so that I can truly experience the presence of God" (*Seeking the Face of God*). In the same book Shannon writes: "It [contemplation] is simply achieving a deep awareness of what always has been and is true of me: namely, that I am in God, as everything that is, is in God."

The image of sunbathing can also help us to understand what contemplative prayer is and how we can go about doing it. When we sunbathe, we lie under the sun and allow its warmth to penetrate our bodies. In sunbathing our only task is to "let it happen," to make ourselves available and vulnerable to the sun and to enjoy its warm touch upon our bodies. So it is with contemplative prayer. Our task is to be open and receptive to the warm touch of God's love. We need do nothing but be receptive to what God offers us. A popular story in prayer circles tells of an old farmer who used to spend a lot of time in church sitting quietly in the presence of the Blessed Sacrament. One day his pastor asked him how he spent his time — what he did while in prayer. The old farmer simply answered, "I look at him and he looks at me." His prayer was one of being available to and enjoying the presence of God.

Every person is born with a potential to contemplate; but, like much else in life, that potential must be nourished and fostered or it will lie dormant. We will now look at three prayers that can help to foster and nourish the contemplative dimension of our being.

PRAYER OF APPRECIATION
FOR GOD'S CREATION

The most natural and perhaps the easiest way for us to develop our contemplative side is by taking time to grow in our awareness and appreciation of God's creation. Our Divine Artist has given us much to admire. An excellent way to thank God for his handiwork is by admiring and appreciating what he has created. When we attend an art festival and take the time to admire a piece of art, we can be sure that our admiration gives the artist pleasure even if we never verbally express our pleasure. The very fact that we take time to look at, touch, and show appreciation for artists' creations establishes a communication between them and us.

So it is when we take time to admire and appreciate God's creation. God is pleased when we stop to gaze at the beauty of a sunrise or sunset, smell a flower, or watch a child at play. The Irish poet, Pádraic Pearse, gives us an example of contemplative appreciation of creation when he writes:

> Sometimes my heart hath shaken with
> Great joy
> To see a leaping squirrel in a tree,
> Or a lady-bird upon a stalk,
> Or little rabbits in a field at evening,
> Lit by a slanting sun. . . .
> Or children with bare feet upon
> The sands
> Of some ebbed sea, or playing on the
> Streets
> Of little towns in Connacht. . . .

Another beautiful description of the human person contemplating the wonder of God's creation is found in Psalm 8. Perhaps one evening the psalmist was out for a stroll, and as he contemplated the star-filled sky, he was filled with awe and wonder. He expressed what was within him in his way:

> O LORD, our Lord, . . .
> When I behold your heavens, the work of your fingers,
>   the moon and the stars which you set in place —
> What is man that you should be mindful of him,
>   or the son of man that you should care for him?
> You have made him little less than the angels,
>   and crowned him with glory and honor. . . .
> O LORD, our Lord,
>   how glorious is your name over all the earth!
> (Psalm 8:2,4-6,10)

Poets and artists have a special talent for expressing their admiration for creation, but God must be equally pleased by our more mundane expressions of delight. By taking time to smell the flowers, behold a sunrise or sunset, or admire a tree, a sea shell, or a painting, we are developing in a very natural way our capacity for contemplative prayer.

CENTERING PRAYER

Centering Prayer is quite popular among Protestant and Catholic Christians alike. Its greatest modern proponent is a Cistercian monk, Father Basil Pennington. He describes it in his book entitled *Centering Prayer: Renewing an Ancient Christian Prayer Form:*

> In Centering Prayer we go beyond thought and image, beyond the senses of the rational mind, to that center of our being where God is working a wonderful work. There God our Father is not only bringing us forth at each moment in his wonderful creative love, but by virtue of the grace of filiation, which we received at Baptism, he is indeed making us sons and daughters, one with his own Son, pouring out in our hearts the Spirit of his Son, so that we can in the fullest sense cry, "Abba Father." He says to us in fact more than in word, "You are my son; this day I have begotten you." At this level of our being where we are our truest selves, we are essentially prayer, total response to the Father in our oneness with the Son, in that love who is the Holy Spirit.

We can read this statement and say, "How beautiful!" But the important point is to *experience* what it says — that is, to actually see ourselves as beloved sons and daughters of the Father and to really feel the indwelling of the Father, Son, and Holy Spirit at our deepest center. Centering Prayer is one of the best means we can use to facilitate the attainment of such an experience. By frequently taking time to find our center point, we gradually, through the grace of God, come to know experientially the Lord who lives in the center of our being, the One who is our deepest center. In centering prayer we become present to the God within and we love him from our deepest center.

How can we learn to pray in this way? Fathers Basil Pennington and Thomas Keating have written extensively about Centering Prayer and how to practice it. The four steps or stages which follow are drawn mainly from their writings.

Stage One: Find a quiet place and take a few minutes to relax. This can be done by slowly inhaling and exhaling. Sitting in a straight-backed chair is the recommended posture for this form of prayer.

Stage Two: Once we feel relaxed, we can make an act of faith to become aware of the presence of God within us. We may wish to pray the following or a similar act of faith:

> Lord Jesus, I believe that you are truly present at the center of my being, bringing me forth in your love. During this prayer period I want to be completely present to you. Draw me into your loving presence and help me to experience myself as your beloved child.

Stage Three: We need to center our whole attention on God, allowing him alone to be the sole concern of our mind and heart. The anonymous author of the fourteenth-century spiritual classic, *The Cloud of Unknowing,* proposes this method:

> This is what you are to do: Lift your heart to the Lord with a gentle stirring of love, desiring him for his own sake and not for his gifts. Center all your attention and desire on him and let this be the sole concern of your mind and heart. Do all in your power to forget everything else, keeping your thoughts and desires free from involvement with any of God's creatures or their affairs whether in general or in particular.

The anonymous author of *The Cloud of Unknowing* is regarded as the originator or creator of the prayer form we call Centering Prayer.

If our mind begins to wander, as it most surely will, it is helpful to choose and use a single word (sometimes called a prayer word or *mantra*) to help us ward off the distractions and keep our minds and hearts on God alone. Many people who practice Centering Prayer choose a prayer word such as peace, love, truth, or Abba. When we are distracted by other images, thoughts, or insights, however noble or spiritual, we should begin to use our prayer word as a means of keeping our entire attention on God. Once focused on God we can allow our prayer word to recede into the background. In other words, we need only use the prayer word to ward off distractions until we once again turn our focus back to God.

Some days we may be so plagued with distractions that we will have to use the prayer word constantly to bring us back on track.

When we sit at the feet of the Lord, he may seem more absent than present. Other days we may be able to stay at the center with little or no effort. It is important that we do not judge a prayer period that is free of distractions as being better and more pleasing to God than a prayer period that has no distractions. A distractionless prayer period is obviously more satisfying but not necessarily more pleasing to God. What God looks for in prayer is a heart that longs for him, seeks him, and cries out for union with him. If we have that thought in prayer, then our prayer, regardless of the number of distractions, is very pleasing to God. Also, when dealing with distractions, we should remember that every decision to turn away from a distraction in order to turn back to God is a decision to love. If during a particular prayer time we turn away fifty times from distractions in order to turn back to God, we can say we have made fifty acts of love. Surely this would be most pleasing to God.

Stage Four: It is suggested that the Centering Prayer period end with a slow recitation of the Lord's Prayer. We may also want to ask the Lord to help us to continue moving through the rest of our day with a sense of God's loving presence.

If we tend to be achievers and doers, we may find Centering Prayer difficult. We may think it is a waste of time and wonder what is the point of just sitting there doing nothing. Centering Prayer is a symbolic way of saying that spiritual growth is the work of God and not of the one who prays. We become holy not so much by our doing but by allowing God to transform us.

THE JESUS PRAYER

The Jesus Prayer is another ancient prayer form that has been rediscovered in recent times. Even though the prayer involves using some words, it can still be considered as a contemplative prayer form. (Contemplative prayer is usually described as a *wordless* form of prayer.) The traditional wording of the Jesus Prayer is this: "Lord Jesus, have mercy on me a sinner." It is based on Luke 18:14 and 18:39. Some people shorten it to "Jesus, have mercy on me" or simply "Jesus." The prayer has been used by Christians — especially Eastern Christian monks — since at least the fourth century. The Fathers of the desert used it to implement

Christ's exhortation to pray without ceasing. Mahatma Gandhi, who was a zealous advocate of this form of prayer, claimed that it brought with it the most extraordinary benefits for spirit, mind, and body. He claimed to have overcome all his fears, even as a child, simply through the ceaseless repetition of God's name. Gandhi has said that there was more power in its recitation than in the atom bomb.

The Jesus Prayer has always been linked with breathing because breath symbolizes the Spirit or life of God within us. As we inhale and say, *"Lord Jesus,"* we can imagine ourselves taking in the love and presence of Jesus and all that is good and beautiful. As we exhale and say, "Have mercy on me a sinner," we can imagine ourselves breathing out of our systems everything that is destructive to our well-being and growth.

While this is one valid way to pray the Jesus Prayer, we should remember that we don't have to synchronize it with our breathing. While some people like to synchronize the prayer with their breathing, others find that this concentration is a distraction. Either way is good. We need only find a formula and rhythm that is good for us.

We can use the Jesus Prayer in both spousal and occupational situations (see pages 40-41). In spousal prayer we will begin our formal time with the Lord by spending a few minutes saying the Jesus Prayer. We take a few moments to "center down" (to become present to the Jesus who dwells with us), and then we begin to rhythmically pray or chant the Jesus Prayer. Many people report that this prayer has a tremendously calming and healing effect on their lives.

In occupational prayer we can also use the Jesus Prayer as we go about the duties of our day. As we drive to work in the morning, we can repeat slowly, "Jesus, have mercy on me," or "Jesus, have mercy on all the people I meet this day." As we go about our work at home or wait in line at the store or at the doctor's office, we can pray the Jesus Prayer. When we participate in meetings that are beginning to produce more heat than light, we can begin to pray the Jesus Prayer. We can pray it when we wake up in the middle of the night. Veteran users of the prayer tell how they actually wake up with this prayer on their lips. It has become one with their breathing. From all this, we can see how regular use of the Jesus Prayer will foster in us a spirit of contemplation.

CONTEMPLATIVE MOMENTS

To conclude this chapter on contemplative prayer, something should be said about what can be called the "gift of a contemplative moment," which is another name for a religious experience. A contemplative moment is the experience of suddenly and spontaneously finding ourselves caught up in the presence of God. Suddenly, unexpectedly, and without perhaps consciously asking for it, we find ourselves loved, embraced, and cherished by God. We have a deep feeling of inner peace and a sense of connectedness with all of creation. Such graced moments may happen as we walk down the street, take a stroll on the beach, sit at our desk, hold a small baby in our arms, sit alone in church, paint a picture, dance, look into a microscope, or whatever. Jesuit Father William Barry gives us two examples of contemplative moments in his book, *God And You*. He writes:

> A man was walking along a beach at night and saw the moonlight touch with silver the crest of a wave. He was delighted and felt at peace and in the presence of someone who himself delights in such things. He felt that God was close and loved him even though he often drank too much and got angry with his family. He knew that God knew all about him and yet loved him, and he felt freer than he had in years.
>
> Recently I was walking near the seashore. It was a bright, crisp autumn day; the sun shone through golden and red leaves and sparkled on the blue water. All of a sudden I felt a tremendous sense of well-being, a great gratitude and a strong desire welling up in me. On reflection I knew that I had felt the touch of God and a strong desire for him.

While such graced moments of contemplation are indeed the free gift of God, we can facilitate their coming by engaging in any of the three examples of prayer outlined in this chapter. These three models of contemplative prayer do indeed facilitate the gift of experiencing communion with God, but we should not be overly concerned with following a particular method. Rather, we should concern ourselves with having a heart that seeks union with its Maker. We should concentrate on creating space in our lives to ponder and be present to the loving presence of God. The extent and quality of our presence to God, the Ground of being, will greatly determine the quality of our presence to people.

REFLECTION QUESTIONS

1. What insight in these pages made the greatest impression on you?
2. Do most people tend to believe that contemplative prayer is only for people in monasteries and not for ordinary Christians? What do you believe?
3. Have you ever experienced a "contemplative moment" as described on page 117, or have you ever tried to contemplate?
4. Did you disagree with or have trouble understanding any part of this section?
5. After doing the suggested prayer exercise that follows, describe your experience.

SUGGESTED PRAYER EXERCISE

Do one of the forms of contemplation offered in this chapter.

12
PRAYING THE
ROSARY CREATIVELY

"Hail, favored one! The Lord is with you. . . . Most blessed are you among women, and blessed is the fruit of your womb."

(Luke 1:28,42)

I have taken to praying the rosary again. It must be a good dozen years since I last prayed in this particular "mode" (as they say), and there is a sense of homecoming . . . about it.

(Mitch Finley)

When I was growing up in the countryside of Ireland (a place dotted with shrines to our Blessed Mother), the family rosary was a must. There was never a valid reason for missing it. If someone was sick in bed, we gathered in that person's room to pray the beads. The family rosary was often said as we all traveled in a car to or from the homes of friends or relatives. My experience was not uncommon. A unique mark of Catholicism was its loyalty to the rosary as a way of honoring Mary and reflecting on the joyful, sorrowful, and glorious events in her Son's life.

But today the rosary is not prayed nearly as much. Many people rejected the rosary as a valid prayer form because they saw it as a mindless, formalized prayer. Yet the rosary has not died. In fact, it is undergoing a revival, as indicated by Mitch Finley's quotation at the beginning of this chapter.

The rosary (which means *rose garden*) has its roots in the Middle Ages. It was seen as a "poor man's breviary" — the breviary (today called the Liturgy of the Hours) being the book from which the clergy prayed the 150 Psalms. The rosary always had close connections with the Scriptures. Since many of the laity in those centuries couldn't read, the strings of Our Fathers were used as a substitute for the breviary. In time, the 150 Our Fathers were reduced to fifteen, but between them a group of ten Hail Marys (called a decade) were prayed. Next, a Glory be to the Father was added after each decade. Finally, the crucifix and the preliminary beads were attached to the original circle of Our Fathers and Hail Marys. Meanwhile, the people continued to reflect on the events in the lives of Jesus and Mary as they prayed their beads. Today these events are called the Mysteries of the Rosary. The fifteen-decade rosary thus consists of the five Joyful, the five Sorrowful, and the five Glorious Mysteries (or events) in the life of Christ and his Mother.

One of the welcome characteristics to the revival of the rosary in our time is that people are bringing much more creativity to the praying of the rosary than before. Mitch Finley, in an article entitled "Recovering the Rosary" (*America,* May 7, 1983), describes one way he prays the rosary:

> Daily, once our three children are off to sleep, when dark has fallen, I take my regular walk around our urban neighborhood. I walk about a mile in one direction, then return by the same route. With beads held in my coat pocket, I walk, rather briskly, and pray. Once I have finished the rosary, I continue grasping the beads but I move over to the Jesus Prayer. Besides family and friends, others pass through my thoughts: those who hunger; those who are tortured or in prison; the strangers in the houses I pass (nearly all gazing into glowing television screens); children who, right here, have been beaten or abused by their beaten and abused parents. The list is, of course, quite endless.

USE CREATIVE APPROACHES

This creative and flexible approach to the rosary is encouraged by the U.S. Conference of Catholic Bishops. In their pastoral entitled *Behold Your Mother: Woman of Faith,* they urge us to adapt the rosary to specific situations:

> Besides the rosary pattern long known to Catholics, we can freely experiment. New sets of mysteries are possible. We have customarily gone from the childhood of Jesus to his Passion, bypassing his whole public life. There is rich matter here for rosary meditation.

What are some ways to act on the bishops' suggestion that we be more creative in our selection of meditations to accompany the praying of the rosary? Perhaps we could use one or some of the following themes:

1. Love Theme

- *First decade:* You are precious in my eyes . . . and I love you (see Isaiah 43:1-5).
- *Second decade:* God loves us like a mother (see Isaiah 49:1,14-16).
- *Third decade:* Jesus washes the feet of his disciples (see John 13:1-15).
- *Fourth decade:* Nothing can separate us from the love of God (see Romans 8:35).
- *Fifth decade:* As the Father loves me, so I also love you (John 15:9).

2. Healing Theme

- *First decade:* Jesus heals us of fear (see Luke 8:22-25).
- *Second decade:* Jesus heals us in our sexuality (see Luke 7:36-50).
- *Third decade:* Jesus heals us of our grief (see Luke 7:11-17).
- *Fourth decade:* Jesus heals us of attachment to riches (see Luke 19:1-10).
- *Fifth decade:* Jesus heals us of self-righteousness (see Luke 18:9-14).

3. Other Themes

There are many other possible themes which could be used to create a set of mysteries: for example, the works of the Holy Spirit, thanksgiving, patience, peace, sin, or mercy. Also, we could just take a phrase or verse of Scripture as a source of meditation as we pray a decade of the rosary. Such phrases or words need not be built around a theme. For example, in preparation for the sacrament of Penance, we could reflect on the following Scriptures:

- *First decade:* Come to me, all you who labor and are burdened, and I will give you rest (Matthew 11:28).

- *Second decade:* I tell you, in just the same way there will be more joy in heaven over one sinner who repents than over ninety-nine righteous people who have no need of repentance (Luke 15:7).
- *Third decade:* While he was still a long way off, his father caught sight of him, and was filled with compassion. He ran to his son, embraced him and kissed him (Luke 15:20).
- *Fourth decade:* As for you, your sins are forgiven (Luke 5:20).
- *Fifth decade:* ''Has no one condemned you?'' Then Jesus said, ''Neither do I condemn you'' (John 8:10-11).

CHOOSE SPECIAL
INTENTIONS FOR EACH DECADE

When we pray the rosary we usually have a particular intention in mind. Sometimes we may pray it for one specific intention; other times we may have one intention for each decade. The following are five intentions that I sometimes use.

- *First decade:* Thanksgiving. I use this decade to give thanks to God for specific things, including thanks for the positive responses to his promptings and callings.
- *Second decade:* Contrition and Healing. I take a moment to reflect on specific ways I failed to respond to God and neighbor. I pray for those who may have been hurt by my sin. I ask God to heal those areas of my life that cause me to do the evil I do and make me fail to do the good I want to do (see Romans 7:15).
- *Third decade:* Intercession. I use this decade to pray for others and their needs, particularly for people I may have encountered during the day.
- *Fourth decade:* Petition. I pray for the specific desires of my own heart.
- *Fifth decade:* Miscellaneous Intentions. I use this decade to pray for specific, current-event happenings in the local or larger world. Notice how this use of the decades of the rosary corresponds to the three steps of the Consciousness Examen (pages 87-89).

Father Joseph Champlin, in *Behind Closed Doors,* writes that he sometimes uses the five decades of the rosary to pray for the people of the five major continents of the world. As he prays each decade, he thinks of the Church and the people on a particular continent, with their needs, burdens, and joys. This way of praying the rosary would certainly give our prayer a universal touch. As we move our way through each bead of the rosary, we meet, as it were, and pray for people all over the world.

The rosary can also be prayed communally during a family gathering, the gathering of several families, or a parish gathering. Mitch Finley, in the same article cited on page 120, describes how he, his wife, and several couples gathered together to pray God's blessing on their marriages. He writes:

> A few weeks ago, my wife and I joined eight other married couples for prayer. We began a series of gatherings to pray for marriage in general, and for marriages in particular — our own and those of couples we know who seem in need of some prayer right about now. A small purpose, really, but one with vast implications.
>
> We lit the living room with fluttering candles and, yes, prayed the rosary — not without self-consciousness, to be sure, since none of us had thought of ourselves as rosary types for a good long time.
>
> What a remarkable thing, I thought to myself. We gathered, greeted one another, and here we are right away praying. We did not spend several meetings trying to agree on how to pray, first.

When such groups gather to pray the rosary, each decade could be preceded with a short reading and concluded with a verse of a sacred song. (Robert and Virginia Broderick's *Pray the Rosary* contains such meditations for fifteen decades of the rosary.)

Saint Paul writes: "Have no anxiety at all, but in everything, by prayer and petition, with thanksgiving, make your requests known to God" (Philippians 4:6). The rosary is certainly one very valid form of prayer that can be used to present our needs to God. If we decide to pray the rosary in some of these creative ways, we may be following the Lord's exhortation by becoming a disciple "who brings from his storeroom both the new and the old" (Matthew 13:52). Spiritual renewal involves, among other things, taking old things out of our spiritual storeroom and using them in new ways that speak to people living in a new age.

REFLECTION QUESTIONS

1. What insight in these pages made the greatest impression on you?
2. What has been your experience with the rosary, past and present?
3. Which, if any, of the above suggestions could enhance your rosary prayer?
4. Did you disagree with or have trouble understanding any part of this section?
5. After doing the suggested prayer exercise that follows, describe your experience.

SUGGESTED PRAYER EXERCISE

Pray the rosary using one of the creative ways suggested in this chapter. Also identify an intention for each decade you pray.

13
PRAYER
IN TIMES OF
SPIRITUAL DRYNESS

The LORD, your God, will circumcise your hearts . . . that you may love the LORD, your God, with all your heart and all your soul, and so may live.

(Deuteronomy 30:6)

If a soul becomes more patient in suffering and readier to endure lack of consolations, this is a sign that it is making greater progress in virtue.

(Saint John of the Cross)

Sooner or later in our prayers we experience what is called *dryness* — a time when we have no sense of God's presence. We may even think we have lost our Beloved or feel abandoned by God. In the school of prayer, few things are more important to understand than the nature and role of spiritual dryness.

There are six significant questions that should be asked about prayer during these desert experiences, as they are sometimes called. Three of these questions will be asked and answered in this chapter. The final three will be dealt with in the next chapter.

Question One: What is it that praying people experience during the desert or dry periods of the spiritual journey?
The actual desert experience will vary depending on the person's level of faith and spiritual maturity. For the beginner in prayer, spiritual dryness frequently means not just the absence of a *felt sense* of the presence of God but also feelings of what Saint Ignatius calls desolation — that is, states of anxiousness, sadness,

or loss of peace flowing from the thought that "I have lost God" or "God has abandoned me."

On the other hand, for the person who is more mature in faith and advanced in the ways of prayer, spiritual dryness may not be an experience of desolation. It will be one which lacks a *felt sense* of God's presence but may be accompanied by the conviction: "Even though I can't feel God's presence (at least on the external level), I do believe the Lord is close and active in my life. Even though I cannot feel his presence (the state of spiritual dryness), I don't feel anxious, sad, or abandoned (the state of desolation). In fact, I feel peaceful." (See *Weeds Among the Wheat* and *When the Well Runs Dry,* by Jesuit Thomas H. Green, for more information on this topic.)

To believe that God is present and active despite his apparent absence can be considered one of the greatest blessings of the spiritual life. For most of us, particularly in the early years of prayer, spiritual dryness usually includes the experience of desolation ("I have lost God; God has abandoned me"). Usually it is a time of spiritual suffering. We think we are getting the "silent treatment" from God. We call out to him all day long, but he never answers (see Psalm 22:3). Spiritual dryness is like journeying in the desert with no water in sight. Prayer is no longer exciting; rather, it is a wearying struggle. Spiritual exercises that once nourished us now are empty, and we have little or no desire to do them.

Another dimension of the desert experience may be a feeling of discouragement as we become keenly aware of our own sinfulness. (We may not yet know that one of the surest signs of growth in the interior life is a growing awareness of our own sinfulness.) We may begin to think we are regressing rather than progressing. We may begin to experience one of the great paradoxes of the spiritual life: The closer we come to God, the farther it seems to us that we are away from him. As we get closer to the all-piercing Light of God, the more our own darkness will show itself. Our lives will appear to be hollow and mediocre. The late Father John Dalrymple, in his book *Simple Prayer,* writes:

> It is as if I were to bring the sleeve of my coat toward the window of the room, and as I move into the light, the dust and dandruff on the sleeve become more obvious. It is not that as I moved the coat got dirtier, but that the light got brighter.

What seems to scare and hurt us most is the thought that we have lost our Beloved and that he has abandoned us (see Song of Songs 3:1-11). This thought or feeling characterizes the experience of desolation described earlier.

To sum up, it can be said that while the actual experience of the desert will be different for different people, for all of us it will mean a *felt sense* of the absence of God. And for those of us whose faith in God is still fragile, it will frequently involve the experience of desolation (the "I have lost God" feeling).

This description of spiritual dryness may give the impression that it is something experienced only by monks, religious, and exceptional lay persons. Yet spiritual directors maintain that this experience is quite common in the lives of many average, prayerful lay people who discover somewhere in the midst of their spiritual journeys that spiritual exercises, which once nourished them immensely now do nothing for them.

Question Two: Why is an understanding of this dimension of prayer so important?

There are at least three reasons why some understanding of spiritual dryness is important.

First, if we do not understand the role of the desert in the spiritual life, we may quit praying in times of dryness. We may think that we have "lost God" and that our prior, positive feelings in prayer were not a gift from God but the creation of our own imaginations. This frequently happens. Many people experience genuine conversion and get all excited about prayer, but they quit when the well runs dry. This is sad because it is often at that time that God wants to do his real work in such persons.

Second, lack of knowledge about the purpose of spiritual dryness may cause us to continue praying in a way that, at *this particular stage* in our spiritual journey, may be more of an obstacle than a help to our spiritual growth. Many people are unaware that at some stage in the spiritual journey God may call them to become less active in prayer so that he can be more active in their spiritual transformation.

Third, the experience of spiritual dryness may either be caused by ourselves or something permitted by God. When it is permitted by God, it is meant to purify us and bring us closer to him. Such dryness is a gift to be accepted and embraced. When spiritual dryness is our doing we need to work at removing the causes of such dryness. Lack of knowledge about the nature and role of spiritual dryness may lead us to believe that a particular experience of dryness in prayer is authentic and God-given when in fact it is something brought on by our own infidelities.

The time of spiritual dryness is a critical time in the spiritual journey. How we respond to it will determine whether we move forward spiritually or make no progress whatsoever.

Question Three: Why does God permit us to experience desert periods in the spiritual journey?

> So I will allure her;
> will lead her into the desert
> and speak to her heart.
> > (Hosea 2:16)

God permits us to experience spiritual desert periods in order to purify us of those things that hinder our spiritual transformation and to teach us some important lessons about the spiritual life and how it works. Here are some specific purifications that God works in us and lessons that he teaches us in the desert experience of prayer.

There are *purifications* to be borne: In the desert God will want to purify us of any excessive attachment we may have to consolation in prayer. If God blesses us in prayer with a multitude of consolations (or "spiritual highs"), there is a danger that we may seek and love "the consolations of our God more than the God of our consolations" (Saint Teresa of Avila). In time of spiritual consolation it is easy to pray. The challenge is to remain faithful to prayer when we experience little or no felt sense of God's presence or action in our lives. During such dry periods God is asking us to love him for himself and not just for the spiritual highs or consolations he offers us in prayer. The Lord is asking us to show that we are not just fair-weather friends but all-weather friends. This kind of purification teaches us that God is to be found more deeply in the desert than in the garden of superficial delights.

At the same time God also wants to purify us of spiritual vanity. John Dalrymple, in his book *Simple Prayer*, explains spiritual vanity in this way:

Someone taking to religion in all zeal, becoming caught up in a campaign of prayer, fasting and spiritual reading, liturgical practice, and retreat weekends might be indulging unawares in one big ego-trip. . . . Conversion of the soul from a worldly life to a spiritual life is at first superficial only. The convert has been given new, spiritual goals; but the conversion is only external; in itself the soul is as full as it ever was of unregenerate tendencies to vanity, arrogance, acquisitiveness, the only difference being that after conversion these tendencies are now attached to spiritual instead of worldly objects. . . . The zeal [of such a person] is infectious, but it is, as yet, chiefly the expression of the person's vanity or self-centeredness, dressed up in Christian clothes.

For God to do his work of spiritual transformation in us, he must purify us of such spiritual vanity. God often brings about this purification by bringing to naught our best efforts to change ourselves and everything and everyone around us. As we sit on the ruins of our self-made temples and projects, we are purified of spiritual vanity and arrogance, and we learn the meaning of spiritual poverty: our complete dependence and need for God to bring about any spiritual growth in others or in ourselves.

In the desert God's intention is not to punish us but to purify us. In the journey of life we consciously or unconsciously become overly attached to persons or objects — so much so that they become idols, and thus more important to us than God. This happened to the Israelites after they lived in the Promised Land for some time. They became so enamored with the blessings of the land that they forgot the One who gave them the land. To purify them of this idolatry God led the Israelites into the desert for a second time where they would be free of all their attachments and free to listen anew to the Word of God (see Hosea 2:16-25.)

There are also several *lessons* to be learned: When God takes away consolation in prayer the first lesson we learn is that God can be encountered at a deeper level than the level of our emotions. God wants to teach us that we are no longer dependent on emotional returns to know we have encountered the Lord. As we grow in our relationship with God, the more we will ''learn to be at home in the dark because we are sure, in faith, that the potter is truly shaping the clay, even though the clay sees nothing of what is happening'' (*When the Well Runs Dry,* by Thomas Green, S.J.).

An example about eating food might help to illustrate this point more clearly. Sometimes we may immensely enjoy eating a delicious meal, savoring every morsel of the food. On another occasion we may not enjoy another type of delicious food. We may not be feeling well, or the food may not appeal to us. Yet from the point of view of nutrition, both meals may be equally good. Our lack of enjoyment of the second meal in no way diminishes its nutritional value.

The same principle is at work in prayer life. Sometimes when we pray we really feel and savor God's presence and love. At other times the prayer is empty and dull. Who, then, are we to say that the latter time is of no benefit to our spiritual growth or is less pleasing in God's sight?

A second lesson God teaches us in the desert is that spiritual consolation is God's pure gift to us and not something we can earn by being good or by praying in a particular way. In prayer God teaches this important lesson by "dropping in" on us when we least expect him and by "failing to show" when we very much want to experience his presence.

A third lesson that God wishes to teach us in the desert is that spiritual growth is totally dependent on God's work in us and not on anything we do. Our task is simply to be flexible and cooperative with the movement of the Spirit. In the spiritual life, "working at it" often means "being still," "just being there," and exercising discipline over our doing and achieving self which so often wants to run the show. This is a difficult lesson for us because so much of our training for the journey of life has told us to be self-sufficient and take-charge individuals. It is not easy for us to switch gears in the inner journey.

In the spiritual life God is the Chief Director: We are the individual unique members of the human cast of billions. Mary, at the Annunciation, is our perfect model (see Luke 1:26-38). When God invites her to become the mother of Jesus, she doesn't respond, "Sure, Lord, *I'll* do it!" Rather, she says, "I am your maidservant; work in and through me as you want." Mary's response was, "Be it done unto me," not, "I'll do it." This attitude is one of active receptivity, and it is the secret of Christian spirituality and spiritual growth. Active receptivity is characterized by the effort to place our energy, will, and freedom at the disposal of God so that he can do with us and in us what he wills.

The final lesson that God teaches us when our prayer runs dry is that we must gradually learn to participate in the Cross of Christ. In times of dryness we are experiencing the thirst of Jesus on the Cross. If the Cross was Jesus' way to the Father, then surely we, the disciples of Jesus, cannot expect to travel the scenic route free of all pain and hardship. When we experience darkness in prayer or in the marketplace, we are being invited to identify with Jesus in his suffering and in his experience of feeling abandoned by the Father. Also, in the desert we are being invited and challenged to trust that our God will not abandon us but will come to rescue us and redeem us (see Exodus 16).

REFLECTION QUESTIONS

1. What insight in these pages made the greatest impression on you?
2. What has been your experience with spiritual dryness in the past?
3. Which of the three lessons mentioned in this chapter helps you the most?
4. Did you disagree with or have trouble understanding any part of this section?
5. After doing the suggested prayer exercise that follows, describe your experience.

SUGGESTED PRAYER EXERCISE

Reflect on some dry periods (or a dry period) in your life. Looking back, can you see any good that came from it? What seemed to be the dominant feeling you had during the dry period: anger, frustration, discouragement, confusion, or anxiety? Were you able to talk to the Lord about such feelings?

14
PRAYER AND
SPIRITUAL DRYNESS
(Continued)

Our hope for you is firm, for we know that as you share in the sufferings [of Christ], you also share in the encouragement.

(2 Corinthians 1:7)

It may be useless — and perhaps a source of still greater agitation — to want to seek assurance that we are in the grace of God and what we are experiencing [a time of spiritual dryness] is only a trial, and not abandonment on the part of God. At such times it is God's will that we should not have this assurance. And he does this so that we may humble ourselves more and increase our prayers and acts of confidence in his mercy. We desire to see, and God wills that we should not see.

(Saint Alphonsus Liguori)

This chapter will continue the treatment of the nature and role of spiritual dryness in the prayer life. There are three more questions that we must ask ourselves about this important topic and they are presented here in the order of their importance.

Question One: How can we tell when a particular desert experience is caused by our own infidelity?

If dryness occurs in prayer, particularly in the early stages when God is giving alternating periods of dryness and consolation, we may tend to blame ourselves for our condition. We may wonder what latest infidelity we committed to bring about this dryness. The fact may be that we have done nothing wrong to occasion it. God may be allowing us to experience it because he wants to purify some aspect of our relationship with him or teach us some spiritual lessons — as we have just seen in the last chapter. On the other hand, we may think the dryness is from God when in fact it is caused by our own laxity and sinfulness. Therefore, it is important that we be able to discern its true cause because our response to it will differ, depending on whether the dryness is something permitted by God or something caused by ourselves.

There are various reasons why we may be the cause of our own spiritual dryness. Here are some of them.

First, we may be indifferent to a sinful pattern of behavior. If we are indifferent to some sinful pattern of behavior in our lives, we can expect difficulty in prayer. In a human friendship, a negative pattern of behavior (a critical or lying spirit, for example), which we make no effort to change, will have a destructive effect on the whole relationship. Likewise, if in our relationship with God, we are deliberately ignoring a sinful pattern of behavior (for example, involvement in an illicit relationship, unforgiveness, or unethical business practices), we can rightfully expect tension in our relationship with God. When we do something like this we are deliberately excluding the Lord and his influence from some area of our lives. In such a situation we should not be surprised that we do not feel God's presence in our times of prayer.

Of course it is important to note that this does not refer to a sinful pattern of behavior that we are trying to change and that we are bringing before the Lord in prayer. In this case we are recognizing sin and struggling with it. Instead of keeping us from God, our struggle with a particular sin or weakness may be the very means that God will use to allow us to experience his love, mercy, and power. Saint Paul's famous example of how his thorn in the flesh became the very means of God's power is an example of this (see 2 Corinthians 12:7-10).

Second, we may be harboring repressed anger at God. Two highly respected spiritual directors, Fathers William Connolly and William Barry, write in their book, *The Practice of Spiritual Direction:* "When prayer flattens out, or appears to be facing an iron wall, the director must always suspect the presence of unexpressed anger." To add to this problem, many of us were raised in a culture where appropriate expression of anger was socially unacceptable. In this vein, the above authors continue: "Hence resentments, holding a grudge or subdued rage, when they are present, are all likely to be given other names like indifference and rational analysis." When others hurt us, our relationship with them diminishes. We may try to cover up by presenting an affable, friendly front; but in reality we will distance ourselves emotionally from them. In a similar way, if we become angry with God about something, we may continue to be faithful to our prayer time, but on an emotional level we can be fairly sure we have distanced ourselves from him. It is important for us to realize that if life is handing us a raw deal, we may well be unconsciously blaming God for our unfortunate situation.

Third, dryness may come as a result of our separating prayer from life. The spiritual life is *all* of life and not just one segment of it. The Lord refuses to be a compartmentalized God; he wants to be part and parcel of our whole life. When we try to keep God in church or in our prayer closet and not allow him to guide all the activities of our day, we can be sure that we are setting ourselves up for dryness in prayer. If we exclude God from the activities of our day, we should not be surprised that he is missing from our prayer time. Even on a human level, no one likes to be a "tag-along" in someone else's life.

Fourth, overwork can lead to dryness. When our prayer life dries up it is good for us to ask if we are pushing ourselves too much on the vital and functional dimensions of life. "Am I overworked? Am I overtired? Am I coming down with the flu? Am I neglecting physical exercise? Do I have a tendency to convert leisure time into work?" These are important questions to ask because their answers affect our prayer life. If we fail to care properly for our bodies, we are neglecting a dimension of ourselves that we depend on to help us to pray. When we are very tired and overworked, prayer may well be seen as just another duty to be performed or something to be done automatically.

Fifth, there may be a lack of honesty in our prayer. Just as shallow or dishonest sharing dulls human relationships, it also dulls the Divine-human relationship. If our prayer is no more than "sweet talk" to "sweet Jesus," we should not expect Jesus to be too interested in our conversation. We must learn to talk to the Lord about the real fabric of our lives.

Sixth, we must avoid half-hearted efforts at prayer. On a human level we may fail to really connect with others because our conversations are just words — words that fail to express what we are truly thinking and feeling. The problem may be that deep down we are scared to encounter each other in a deep way. When a relationship is characterized by this type of communication, we should expect it to be empty and unfulfilling. In a similar vein, when our prayer time consists mainly of the rote recitation of certain prayers or of inattentive spiritual reading — when we merely *say* prayers and *perform* acts of piety with no real desire to encounter God and grow in relationship with the Lord — we should expect little or no satisfaction in prayer. In fact, our spiritual exercises may become a substitute for a real relationship with God.

If we discern that *we* are the cause of our spiritual dryness, we should do all we can to remove the particular obstacle. For example, if the problem is that we are holding onto a grudge and doing nothing to let it go, we may need to pray the prayer of forgiveness suggested in Chapter Six or we may need to speak openly to the person with whom we are having a problem. If we discern that our experience of spiritual dryness is due to our tendency to separate prayer from life, our solution will be to work at allowing the Lord to walk with us in all the activities of our day. (Key Three and Chapter Seven should help to resolve this obstacle to intimacy with God.)

In short, when we discern that we ourselves are the cause of the spiritual dryness, we ought to do something to remove the obstacle. Judging from the experience of most, if not all, disciples of the Lord, once we begin to struggle with an obstacle, prayer again becomes alive and we experience a new closeness to God. Of course, in trying to discern the cause of our spiritual dryness, it would be well to seek the counsel of a good spiritual director. Most of us tend to think that spiritual dryness is due to some infidelity on our part. The truth may be that God is permitting us to experience the desert so that he can continue his purifying work in us — which leads us directly to the next question.

Question Two: What indications do we have that God might be permitting our spiritual dryness to continue his purifying work within us?

While we can never be absolutely sure — since we live by faith and not by clear vision — when spiritual dryness is being permitted by God, we can say that the following are good indications that the dryness is the purifying work of God:

- If during the time of dryness we remain faithful to prayer.
- If our prayer is honest and flows from the real fabric of our lives.
- If we are trying to integrate prayer and life.
- If we are trying to live a life of charity; if our prayer helps us to be more loving.
- If we are genuinely trying to avoid sin and live our lives according to God's Word.
- If we thirst for God as we walk in the desert.

It is crucial to remember that *our desire* for God is in itself a tangible sign of his presence in our lives. We couldn't even desire God if he didn't place that desire in our hearts.

Prayer, like so many other aspects of life, is a series of "arrivals" and "starting points." We arrive at a point where we feel good. We experience the grace of consolation. But that lasts only a little while and then a certain discontent (a kind of desert) sets in — a discontent that may be caused by ourselves or permitted by God. Then we are faced with the challenge of discerning who is causing the discontent: "Is it God or me?" The purpose of the discontent caused by God is to create in us a longing for more, to create in us a desire to move closer to the Lord. In the spiritual journey God brings us to a particular point or state; he lets us rest there and enjoy that plateau for a little while, and then he says, "Okay. Let's move ahead and seek for more" (see Exodus 40:36-37). Of course, it is not easy to move when we are not sure where he is leading us. All he says is, "Move, and trust that I'll take you to a new and better place." If our thoughts, words, or actions are the cause of dryness and discontent, it is necessary for us — with God's guidance — to chart a new cause for our spiritual life.

In summary, if we are in doubt about the cause of our discontent or dryness, we should talk to a spiritual guide or, if that is not possible, simply say a prayer like this: "Lord, if this dryness I am experiencing is due to some failing of mine, please reveal it to me. Until you do, I am going to assume that I am not the cause of the dryness."

Question Three: What are some measures we can take to help sustain us in our spiritual dryness?

There are four measures available.

First, we should find a wise spiritual director. A wise spiritual director is one who understands the role of the desert in the spiritual life and hopefully one who has experienced and grown through the desert experience in his or her own spiritual journey. Many people whom God led into the desert for purification have suffered much at the hands of well-intentioned but misinformed spiritual guides. (Saint John of the Cross reserves some of his harshest words for this type of spiritual director.) A misinformed guide, for example, may insist that we continue to meditate and double our spiritual reading when God is actually calling us to the prayer of contemplation.

A good desert-experienced spiritual director will always be a source of guidance, encouragement, and inspiration. That is why — when we are spiritually dry — it is so important that we find and place our trust in a good and wise director. But, as most of us know, wise spiritual directors are nearly as scarce as palm trees in Alaska. The truth is that the road to authenticity is dangerous, hard, and narrow, and few decide to travel it. In the absence of a wise spiritual director (and there is really no substitute for such a person), we may receive some guidance from books that are written or recommended by people who are recognized guides of the inner journey.

Second, we need to maintain a strong faith. This will enable us to believe that:

- God knows what he is doing when he allows us to experience the desert (see Romans 11:33-36);
- In the desert God is not punishing us but is purifying us (see Deuteronomy 30:6);
- God grows his best flowers (virtues) in the desert (see Hosea 2:1-11);
- God works in us while we rest in him (see Mark 4:26-29);
- In the struggles of life God is on our side fighting our battles (see Exodus 14:13-14 and Deuteronomy 1:30-33);
- In the desert God's seeming absence is just a different type of presence, one that we may not as yet have recognized (see Exodus 16);

- We can be secure with insecurity (see Romans 8:28);
- We should abandon ourselves generously to the purifying work of God (see Luke 23:46).

Third, we should remain faithful to prayer. In the desert, prayer is usually dry and therefore we find it difficult to remain faithful to it. For this reason, spiritual guides counsel us to avoid two extremes or temptations. The first temptation is to quit prayer, thinking that our best efforts are leading us nowhere. The second is to overload our prayer time with extra prayers, rosaries, Scripture reading, and more. It is not helpful to think that if we try harder we will once more feel the presence of God. This second temptation needs to be resisted not only because it blocks God's purpose in the desert but also because it is (usually unconsciously) our attempt to remain active and in control of the prayer process.

In general, prayer in the desert leads us to be much less active and much more passive — less us, more God. The desert challenge involves learning to sit quietly in the presence of God, trusting that he is at work in us while we rest in him. Learning to "waste time and do nothing" in prayer is, without a doubt, one of the most difficult lessons we have to learn in the school of prayer. Unfortunately, most of us never learn to waste time gracefully in the presence of God. Such a practice goes completely against our Western, work-ethic nature — a nature that drives us to do, to achieve, and to produce. We are conditioned not to be satisfied until we see tangible results for our efforts. Because of this need, most of us fill the vacuum that we feel in the desert with reading or prayers of some sort. For those of us who are willing to try to do less (that is, to be less active) in prayer so that God may do more in us, the following suggestions might be helpful.

- Spend some time just being present with the Lord, aware that as we rest in him he is at work in us. Put aside all effort to achieve "success" in prayer and realize that achievement (growth) is God's work.
- Spend some time slowly repeating prayers like: "Incline my heart to your will, O Lord." "Make me want you, O Lord, more than anyone/anything in my life."

- Take a phrase of Scripture like, "You are my beloved Son," and dwell on it.
- Take one word like "Jesus" or "love" and repeat it gently and slowly, letting God do the work, leading us beyond conceptual thoughts, images, or feelings to wordless depths.
- Be present with Mary after she lost Jesus (see Luke 2:41-50) and at the foot of the cross (see John 19:25-27), which must have been a real dark night of the spirit for her. Then ask Mary to intercede for us so that we may have something of the faith which she had when she thought she had lost Jesus.
- Read something on spiritual dryness. Reading and rereading portions of a book like Father Green's *When the Well Runs Dry* will encourage us to persevere in the desert.

When we pray we must place ourselves at God's disposal. What actually happens at prayer is God's business. This piece of wisdom should help to free us from thinking that it is up to us to make things happen in prayer. Once we relax, knowing that our role is to be faithful in coming aside, we can eliminate distractions from within and without and pray as we feel led. ("Pray as you can, not as you can't.") The rest is in God's hands. If God chooses to bless us with a deep sense of his presence, we should indeed be very grateful. If the Lord chooses to bless us with his *seeming* absence (God is always only *seemingly* absent), we should try to be grateful for that — because we believe that God knows what will best help us to grow. According to Father John Dalrymple, "Our prayer is good when our hearts are fixed on God, even if it is filled with boring aridity or passionate turmoil."

Fourth, we should seek the support of fellow pilgrims. While each person's inner journey is very personal and unique, much can be learned from the journeys of co-pilgrims. Only the foolish try to travel the inner journey alone. In the desert we are all beggars sharing morsels of bread with each other. Also, if we are blessed enough to be part of a small, faith-sharing group, we have available to us an excellent resource for the dry times. In the dry times the prayers of fellow pilgrims are usually a big help.

Finally, this prayer of Father Henri Nouwen, taken from his book, *A Cry for Mercy: Prayers from the Genesee,* can be a source of great encouragement during times of spiritual dryness and desolation:

Dear Lord, in the midst of much inner turmoil and restlessness, there is a consoling thought: maybe you are working in me in a way I cannot yet feel, experience or understand. My mind is not able to concentrate on you, my heart is not able to remain centered, and it seems as if you are absent and have left me alone. But in faith I cling to you. I believe that your Spirit reaches deeper and further than my mind or heart, and that profound movements are not the first to be noticed.

Therefore, Lord, I promise I will not run away, not give up, not stop praying, even when it all seems useless, pointless, and a waste of time and effort. I want to let you know that I love you even though I do not feel loved by you, and that I hope in you even though I often experience despair. Let this be a little dying I can do with you and for you as a way of experiencing some solidarity with the millions in this world who suffer far more than I do. Amen.

REFLECTION QUESTIONS

1. What insight in these pages made the greatest impression on you?
2. Has this chapter helped you discover some possible reasons why you suffer spiritual dryness at times?
3. What measures do you take to help you persevere in the desert?
4. Did you disagree with or have trouble understanding any part of this section?
5. After doing the suggested prayer exercise that follows, describe your experience.

SUGGESTED PRAYER EXERCISE

As suggested in this chapter, seek the support of co-pilgrims in your efforts to overcome periods of desolation. Learn from them different ways to cope with desert experiences.

15
SMALL-GROUP
SCRIPTURAL PRAYER

When they entered the city they went to the upper room where they were staying, Peter and John and James and Andrew, Philip and Thomas, Bartholomew and Matthew, James son of Alphaeus, Simon the Zealot, and Judas son of James. All these devoted themselves with one accord to prayer, together with some women, and Mary the mother of Jesus, and his brothers.

(Acts 1:13-14)

Joining fully with sisters and brothers in worship . . . neutralizes a tendency toward excessive self-centeredness and fosters a spirit of charity, of love reaching out toward others.

(Joseph M. Champlin)

Small-group sharing of Scripture and spontaneous prayer is a relatively new development in the prayer life of many Catholics. Yet the Scriptures showed that this type of prayer was very normal for the first followers of Jesus. They frequently gathered together to share the Word of God and to pray together (see Acts 2:42). Despite this experience of the early Church, few twentieth-century Catholics experienced the sharing of Scripture and spontaneous prayer as a part of their earlier spiritual formation. When Catholics prayed with others, they usually used formal or ''learned'' prayers like those used in the rosary or at novenas.

Of course such formal prayers and devotions still have their value and place, but today the Lord is showing us a different kind of prayer and it behooves us to be open and receptive to this new movement of the Spirit. Countless numbers of Catholic Christians now gather together in each other's homes to share Scripture, their personal faith journeys, and to pray together. This new development can enrich not only our relationship with God, but it can also bring new enrichment and depth to our relationships with others. There are many reasons for this.

Listening to how others interpret Scripture passages and how they approach God in prayer can inspire, challenge, and teach us many things. As we learn how others trust God in seemingly impossible situations, we are inspired to do the same. As we listen to stories of healing and reconciliation, we are inspired and challenged to reach out to God with greater faith. As we listen to others pray with conviction and boldness, we are encouraged to do the same. Sharing prayer with others can be a spiritually enriching experience for us, challenging us to pray in ways we never prayed before. In other words, small-group sharing prayers allow us to receive much informal spiritual direction.

The very act of praying out loud and verbalizing our faith stories with others usually deepens our religious beliefs and helps to make God more real and personal.

Also, when we are experiencing spiritual dryness, the prayer and support of others can help us immensely. We may, at first, have no desire to attend a small-group sharing session, but when the meeting is over we may be glad we attended. The faith and prayer of the others may well uplift our downcast spirit.

In and through small-group faith sharing we can receive much spiritual guidance for our lives. As we listen to the simple sharings of others, God may speak a word of direction to us for our unique spiritual journey.

Small-group faith sharing can also enrich our human relationships. When we reveal our spiritual selves, we are sharing the deepest part of our being; this usually brings about the deepest level of intimacy. Honest, spontaneous prayer can create an atmosphere that leads to the sharing of ourselves in ways that otherwise may not have taken place.

The experience of common, shared prayer can be a tremendous support to us as we travel life's journey. Praying and sharing with others about the joys, sorrows, and struggles of life can replace much of the loneliness and isolation of life with feelings of support and of being on the spiritual journey together.

SUGGESTED FORMAT
FOR SHARING PRAYER

As with every form of prayer, each group will have to discover the format that best suits the personalities and needs of its members. Several suggestions are offered here that could be used in a small-group sharing situation. Those who are interested in this type of prayer may decide to use some of these suggestions; others may wish to omit some of them; and still others may want to add some of their own.

Step One: Begin with a song. A good, lively song or two usually helps us get out of our own preoccupations and become part of a community whose purpose is prayer. If a particular group is not the singing type, it is possible just to listen to a sacred song or simply spend a few minutes quieting down and relaxing in the loving presence of God. The aim in this first step is to move our focus off ourselves and onto the Lord. Of course, later on in the session we may want to speak to the Lord and to the group about our preoccupations or concerns. But initially our aim should be to focus on the Lord and become aware of his movement in our midst.

Step Two: Spend a few minutes praising and thanking God for his goodness and blessings. Instead of beginning by focusing on what we want — asking God to give us this and that — we can seek to identify our blessings and God's goodness to us. This also creates a positive and grateful spirit in the group. If the group has little or no experience with shared prayer, it is best to begin by offering brief and simple prayers to God. Long, fancy prayers can be intimidating. Begin with a prayer like this:

> Lord, I thank you for a good day at the office. I thank you for my loving spouse and children. I thank you, Lord, for helping me in my relationship with so-and-so. I thank you also for these brothers and sisters gathered here.

Step Three: Spend time seeking God's mercy for our failings. Having thanked God for his love, we can take some time to express our sorrow for the ways that we failed to respond to his love. "Confession is good for the soul," as the saying goes. Rather than foolishly carrying around our failures, it is wise and healthy to name them and give them to the Lamb of God who is in our midst to take away the sins of the world. Saint James writes: "Therefore, confess your sins to one another and pray for one another" (James 5:16). Confession and repentance of sin lead to spiritual and psychological healing.

In the Gospel of Mark, Jesus points out the vital importance of bringing a forgiving heart to prayer: "When you stand to pray, forgive anyone against whom you have a grievance, so that your heavenly Father may in turn forgive you your transgressions" (Mark 11:25). For a group of people who do not know each other, this part of the prayer may be the most difficult but also the most rewarding. While there is no need to go into details about our sins, it is healthy to acknowledge our failings and not to gloss over our sinfulness or rationalize it away.

At all times during shared prayer — especially during this step — we should make sure that we speak in the first person singular. We are not there to confess the sins of other people. Rather than saying, "Lord, forgive us for the times that we get a *little* mad with each other," pray instead, "Lord, forgive me for the inappropriate way I expressed my anger at so-and-so yesterday." Such a prayer is personal, concrete, and brief.

Step Four: Read and share a Scripture text. The group may now decide to share personal reflections on a particular text of Scripture. The sharing may focus on one passage or incident or on a whole chapter. Ideally the group will know from the previous meeting which text is to be shared and will have reflected on it during the week.

This part of the evening should begin with a slow, deliberate reading of the Scripture to be shared. After the text is read, someone might say a short prayer to the Holy Spirit, asking for inspiration to reveal the meaning of this Word for the life of each person. The leader then invites the members of the group to share personal reflections. This sharing should be at a heart level — what the text personally says to each person — as opposed to a head-type sharing where individuals share in an intellectual and scholarly way. The aim of this activity is not to get into a heady discussion about the scholarly meaning of the particular text. A period of shared prayer is far different from a Bible study situation.

Shared prayer does not permit group members to examine the merits and demerits of a particular person's sharing. Rather, we should simply share how a particular text spoke to us and challenged us on a personal level.

Each person's sharing should be accepted and appreciated — even though we may not agree with it. Also, we should not get into a discussion about a particular sharing. Ideally, one person shares and then the group pauses for a moment to allow the others to reflect on that insight. After that, each person who wishes may go through the same sharing process.

As we ponder the text prior to the prayer group meeting in preparation for a fruitful sharing of God's Word, we might ask ourselves the following questions:

• What do I think this Word of God is saying to me?
• What part of this text spoke to me most?
• How does this text touch my life?
• What does this text ask of me?
• What will it cost me?

To illustrate more concretely the type of sharing envisioned here, consider the story about the cure of the blind man of Jericho from the Gospel of Mark.

> And as he [Jesus] was leaving Jericho with his disciples and a sizable crowd, Bartimaeus, a blind man, the son of Timaeus, sat by the roadside begging. On hearing that it was Jesus of Nazareth, he began to cry out and say, "Jesus, son of David, have pity on me." And many rebuked him, telling him to be silent. But he kept calling out all the more, "Son of David, have pity on me." Jesus stopped and said, "Call him." So they called the blind man, saying to him, "Take courage; get up, he is calling you." He threw aside his cloak, sprang up, and came to Jesus. Jesus said to him in reply, "What do you want me to do for you?" The blind man replied to him, "Master, I want to see." Jesus told him, "Go your way; your faith has saved you." Immediately he received his sight and followed him on his way.
>
> (Mark 10:46-52)

Having read the text, we should pray to the Holy Spirit, asking for understanding of this Word and for insight on how each person should hear and act upon it. Next, we should silently wait for a member of the group to begin sharing on the text. One person might say: "What struck me most about this text was the determination of the blind beggar to gain the attention of Jesus. I was impressed by how he refused to be put off by the crowd who scolded him. That part of the passage made me realize how I often lack the same determination to reach Jesus. It also made me realize how I allow the critical voice of the crowd to hinder me from becoming a more dedicated disciple of Jesus. As a result of praying this text, I have become more aware of how the negative words of others can cause me to pull back in my own efforts to be a dedicated disciple of Jesus."

After a sharing like this, the group should pause for a moment to allow the shared words to enter their hearts. Then a second person can begin to share. This person's sharing might sound something like this: "I was struck by how Jesus invited the crowd to participate in the healing of the blind man. The text reveals that after Jesus called to Bartimaeus, the crowd told the man that the Master wanted to see him and that he had nothing to fear. In this situation the crowd was supportive, and they helped the man in need to come to Jesus. I was struck by that, and it made me ponder how Jesus wants me to bring others to him and to bring his healing to others. I felt challenged by the text because by nature I am quiet and private in my faith. I would really have to stretch myself if I were to become an active instrument of God in leading others to his Son Jesus." Again, after this sharing the group would pause for a moment before moving on to the next person.

In this format each person who wishes to share his or her prayerful reflections should be given the opportunity to do so. Of course, no one should be pressured into sharing.

During the sharing a member of the group might raise some questions about the text. One person might ask: "I'd love to have the faith and determination of Bartimaeus. How can I grow in this type of faith?" Another might ask: "How can I stop being hindered by the words of others that keep me from being a better disciple?" It seems best to respond to such questions after each person has had an opportunity to share his or her reflections on the text. Otherwise, the group may get bogged down in a discussion of the text. In all this, it is important to note that the quality of the sharing will depend a great deal on the amount of preparation made by each participant.

Step Five: Take a few minutes to offer spontaneous prayer based on the text and the reflections shared. Having spent some time talking to each other about the Scriptures and how they relate to our personal spiritual journeys, we can now begin to talk to God about all that we have shared. Our prayer can be very simple and direct; it may take a variety of forms. We may feel led to thank God, to petition him, or simply to rest quietly in his presence. If there are periods of silence during this step, we should try to be relaxed and not feel like we have to say something.

Step Six: Spend some time sharing life experiences. The purpose of this step is to give participants an opportunity to share the joys, sorrows, and struggles of their everyday lives. This step assumes that the members of the group are beginning to feel comfortable with each other and are willing to share some of the intimate feelings of their lives and how they sense these feelings are connected to the gospel. This step, when properly facilitated, can be tremendously rewarding; but when poorly facilitated, it can present some real difficulties.

For example, a person may share happenings from his or her life that should be more appropriately shared with a confessor or counselor. Normally, a meeting such as this is not a place "to tell it all." This is not to say that one shouldn't share deeply. Unless we share some real facts about our lives, this step will be very unreal and superficial. Regarding what is appropriate and inappropriate for sharing with the group, there are no simple, clear-cut guidelines. Each group will have to "feel its way" and gradually discover, through trial and error, what is appropriate for its members.

Another potential difficulty is the response made to what is shared. There is the danger that group members will become judgmental, that they will respond with a list of "shoulds," or that they will be so loving and accepting that the person sharing is offered no challenge. The group's task is not to offer solutions to problems that surface but to help each participant understand more clearly God's strength and ways.

The difficulty inherent in this kind of sharing is such that any group venturing into deep sharing of personal lives would be wise to seek the help of someone skilled in the dynamics of small-group interaction.

For several years I have belonged to a small group of priests who gather together once a month to share faith and life. At one point we realized that as a group we were "stuck" and not going anywhere. We enlisted the help of an outsider with skills in group dynamics. The mere presence of our guest facilitator brought more discipline to the group. Also, his expertise in group dynamics gave us added confidence and a sense of security that allowed us to share what we ordinarily wouldn't share. He also modeled for us the kinds of ways we might respond to one another as we shared some painful area of our lives.

This step, when properly facilitated, will be of great benefit to the group's human and spiritual growth. Ideally, this kind of small-group experience should be both supportive and challenging.

Step Seven. Conclude with some prayers of petition. Group sharing can end with a period of spontaneous prayer based on the sharings from Step Six, on the needs of the group, and on the needs of the larger Church and world. Sometimes the group may decide to pray with each person, letting each person have an opportunity to express his or her needs. People who experience such prayer usually find it comforting, supportive, and strengthening.

REFLECTION QUESTIONS

1. What insight in these pages made the greatest impression on you?
2. Has this chapter helped you to be more open in your faith sharing?
3. Which two of the above steps do you consider essential for a good faith-sharing group?
4. Did you disagree with or have trouble understanding any part of this section?
5. After doing the suggested prayer exercise that follows, evaluate your experience.

SUGGESTED PRAYER EXERCISE

If you are presently active in a small, faith-sharing group and are not using some of the steps mentioned in this chapter, choose one or two of those steps, make them a part of your sharing for a couple of weeks, and see what happens.

CONCLUSION

God very much desires each of us to come to the point where we look forward to spending time with the Lord and feeling at ease in his presence. God doesn't want us to be constantly anxious and insecure about our relationship with him; and he does not want us to see prayer (our time with God) as something we think we must do if we are to make it to heaven. Who of us would like to have a friend who relates to us only because he or she feels some obligation to do so? Yet, too often, isn't that the way we see our relationship with God? Frequently addressing God in prayer is treated as another obligation to which we have to attend.

When we come to the point of praying because we want to spend time with God, we have been given a great grace. It is a grace that all of us should pray for on a regular basis. We could pray that we can make our own the longing for God of which the psalmist wrote:

> O God, you are my God whom I seek;
> for you my flesh pines and my soul thirsts
> like the earth, parched, lifeless and without water.
>
> (Psalm 63:2)

If we normally want to spend time with God, the way to go about it will be relatively simple. In our human friendships, two very important questions need to be asked: "Do the persons seeking to relate really want to be with each other? Do they normally like each other?" If they do not want to be together and do not like each other, their best efforts to relate will fail. On the other hand, if they sincerely like each other's company and are committed to being friends, it will be easy enough for them to find ways, times, and places to be together. They may do this in various ways: by going for a walk, by attending a movie, by eating out together or just sitting at home together. They may contact each other early in the morning or late at night. At times their contact with each other may be either a quick "hello" on the phone or a long, in-depth conversation. Sometimes one party may do nearly all the talking while the other listens patiently.

As it is with our friends, so it is, or should be, between God and us. If God is someone we truly want to befriend, we will not have a big problem discovering ways, times, and places to express our relationship with the Lord.

We can spend time with God in countless ways: by talking, listening to the Word, praising, thanking, repenting, petitioning, complaining, weeping, seeking guidance, waiting for revelation, admiring creation, praying the rosary, singing, dancing, reading, or just resting in the Lord's presence. The main point is that we are sincerely trying to be there for and with the Lord. The central idea is wanting to be with God and wanting to be sensitive and responsive to the Lord's promptings; the rest is secondary.

Also, we should feel free to reach out to God at any time and in any place. At times our contact with him will be like a brief phone call in which we say: "Hi, I love ya!" "Help! I 'goofed'; forgive me." "Wow, what a sunrise this morning; it was great!"

There will be times when our conversations are more in-depth: We'll talk about serious personal problems or we'll take extra time to do spiritual reading, journaling, or contemplation. The important point is that we don't leave our contact with God to chance. It is good to pray when we feel like it. But if we pray only when we feel like it, there is a real chance that God may get the leftover scraps of our day. No one likes to get the leftover scraps of another person's day, especially when that person is considered to be a friend.

If we look to God as a friend, we will make sure that time with him is part of our daily schedule and not something left to chance. We will be certain that our contact with God is more than the quick phone calls that are made as we run from one engagement to another. Of course, some people's circumstances in life will leave them much more time to pray. God understands each of our situations and is willing to work within our limitations.

To repeat, the important point is *wanting* to spend time with God and proving that by frequently connecting with him as we move through the day. The how, where, and when of our prayer is a secondary issue. What really matters is that we have a heart that truly seeks him. "Yes, when you seek me with all your heart, you will find me with you . . . " (Jeremiah 29:13-14). What matters is that we have a heart that seeks to be filled with God's love and that seeks to be a channel of that love to all of creation.

Your Comments Are Welcome

Father Tobin would appreciate any thoughts that you may wish to offer on what has been written here. What did you like about the book? If you used the book with a small group, how was that experience for you? If the book were being revised, what changes or additions would you suggest? Please mail your comments to:

Father Eamon Tobin
c/o Liguori Publications
Books and Pamphlet Department
One Liguori Drive
Liguori, Missouri 63057-9999

APPENDIX

HOW TO
USE THIS BOOK FOR
SMALL-GROUP DISCUSSION

A small-group discussion of a book invariably leads to a deeper understanding and appreciation of the contents. In sharing our reflections on the contents of a book, we can point out to each other some details that we would otherwise have missed. The actual verbalization of our responses to the questions at the end of each chapter and our listening to the other participants' reflections will lead to a greater clarity and depth of understanding of the subject matter.

When we participate in a small-group discussion of a book, we often receive helpful insights and personal experiences related to the topic. In short, the shared reflections of several people who have read a book together usually provide a much richer experience than just a private reading of the material.

SUGGESTED FORMAT

The following is a simple, three-step format that a small group could use to reflect together on the contents of this book.

Step One: Opening Prayer
Each group should decide on the type of opening prayer that best suits its members and prepares their hearts for an open discussion of the book. One group might begin with a brief period of shared, spontaneous prayer; another group may decide to begin with a decade of the rosary; and still another group may decide to assign a different person each week to prepare an opening prayer or brief

prayer service. If the group decides to begin each session with a brief prayer service, the person preparing the service may wish to keep two points in mind:

- The prayer leader should create an opening prayer service that has as its theme the topic to be discussed.
- The opening prayer service might include the following elements: a song sung by the group or played on a tape recorder, a Scripture or nonscriptural reading, a brief reflection on the reading, and a short prayer.

As part of the opening service, the participants could say this prayer together each week:

Father, we thank you for gathering us together for this time of sharing and reflection. Open our hearts to your Holy Spirit who is present and active in each of us. Help us to share our thoughts, feelings, and experiences. Help us also to listen with love and respect to one another. Above all, Father, bind us together in love and help us to be clear channels of your wisdom for one another. This we ask through Christ our Lord. Amen.

Step Two: Discussion of the Contents

After the opening prayer service the group leader or facilitator can begin the discussion by inviting the participants to share their reflections on the material that was assigned or on the questions listed at the end of the assigned reading. After the first week the group leader might want to begin each session by asking: "Does anyone have anything to add to our sharing from last week?" Asking this question gives the group an opportunity to hear how a particular participant might have put into practice an insight or bit of wisdom that was shared the previous week. Also, the question gives the group an opportunity to deal with any unfinished business from the previous week.

Group leaders should feel free to rearrange or adjust the chapters, reflection questions, and prayer exercises offered by the author. For example, a group may decide to discuss two chapters each time they meet, or they might decide to omit some chapters due to a time limitation. Also, the group leader may offer the participants some reflection questions or prayer exercises other than those offered by the author. The important point to keep in mind is to be creative, adaptive, and not overly rigid in the format chosen.

Step Three: Summing Up and Closing Prayer

Once again, each group should decide on a closing prayer form that suits the needs of its participants. Here are two suggestions.

First, have a brief time of silent reflection so that each participant will have an opportunity to discern what message or word God spoke to him or her through the small-group sharing. The message received may come from a personal experience shared by a fellow participant rather than from anything contained in the contents of the book. After the period of silent reflection, the leader may want to give each participant an opportunity to state in one sentence the personal message that he or she has resolved to pursue. It is suggested that each participant be invited by name to share that message with the others. This may be the only time that some quiet or silent participants may share their insights with the group. Of course, even in this situation each person should feel free to share or to say nothing.

Second, the closing prayer could take a different format and give participants an opportunity to mention prayer intentions for themselves and others.

ROLE OF THE GROUP FACILITATOR

The role of the facilitator is to keep the participants on the topic that they are discussing. The facilitator also prevents any one or two people from dominating the exchange by encouraging all participants to share both their thoughts and their personal experiences.

In the initial stages of a small-group experience, especially when the participants do not know one another, there may be a tendency for the facilitator to consciously, but more often unconsciously, take on the role of "answer-person" or "group expert." The participants themselves may unconsciously place the group leader in that role. It is crucial for the group leader not to allow himself or herself to become the "answer-person" or "dominant talker." This is particularly important in a discussion of a book on prayer when everyone will have insights and experiences to share. No one individual should present himself or herself as expert or teacher of the rest. If people are looking for lectures or mini-sermons on prayer, most likely they will go somewhere other than a small group to have that need met.

If facilitators find that the participants have a tendency to look to them for all the answers, they can deal with this potential problem by simply asking, "Can anyone help (name of participant) with that question?"

It should also be noted that the role of the facilitator occasionally involves helping the participants evaluate their small-group experience in the course of a meeting. This evaluation can be done by asking the participants to respond to the following questions:

- What has been helpful or good about our shared experience thus far?
- What has not been helpful or what has been frustrating or hindering the process?
- Is there anything we can do to enrich the group experience?

The facilitator may need to encourage the participants to be honest in their evaluation of how the process is working. In one-to-one or group relationships, "being nice" and saying only what people want to hear may facilitate harmony, but it will also bring on stagnation. On the other hand, giving constructive criticism may be a risk; but where there is openness, this invariably brings about growth and improvement in the group process.

HOW TO BE
A GOOD PARTICIPANT

The degree of openness and participation by the members of a small group will determine to a great extent the quality of the experience for all the participants.

Participants will enrich a small-group process by:

- reading beforehand the assigned pages for each meeting in a prayerful and reflective manner;
- sharing their thoughts, feelings, or personal experiences of the subject matter;
- actively listening when other participants share their reflections;

- encouraging and affirming participants who tend to hesitate to share;
- trying to keep the group focused on the topic;
- offering an honest evaluation of the group process when invited to do so;
- praying for the spiritual success and growth of the group.

Participants will hinder and obstruct the small-group process by:

- failing to prepare the assignment for each meeting;
- complaining and using the small-group discussion to air their pet peeves;
- rambling and talking off the topic;
- harshly criticizing the reflections of others;
- dominating the discussion by acting as if they have a monopoly on the Holy Spirit;
- offering only heady remarks and rarely, if ever, sharing a personal experience;
- never participating in the sharing process.

It would be wise for the facilitator to have the participants reflect on these characteristics of helpful and unhelpful participants after the opening prayer of the first session. It might also be helpful to review this section after a few sessions, particularly if the facilitator thinks some of the group seem to show evidence of being unhelpful participants.

BIBLIOGRAPHY

Alphonsus Liguori, Saint. *To Love Christ Jesus*. Edited by Nancy Fearon, I.H.M., and Christopher Farrell, C.SS.R. Liguori, MO: Liguori Publications, 1987.

Anonymous. *The Cloud of Unknowing*. Translated by William Johnson, S.J. Garden City, NY: Doubleday, 1973.

Aschenbrenner, George, S.J. "Consciousness Examen." *Review for Religious*. Vol. 31, No. 1 (January, 1972).

Barry, William, S.J. *God and You*. Mahwah, NJ: Paulist Press, 1988.

Brissette, Claire M. *Reflective Living: A Spiritual Approach to Everyday Life*. Whitinsville, MA: Affirmation Books, 1983.

Champlin, Joseph M. *Behind Closed Doors*. Mahwah, NJ: Paulist Press, 1984.

Connolly, William, and William Barry. *The Practice of Spiritual Direction*. New York, NY: Harper and Row, 1982.

Dalrymple, John. *Letting Go in Love*. Wilmington, DE: Michael Glazier, Inc., 1987.

_____. *Simple Prayer*. Wilmington, DE: Michael Glazier, Inc., 1984.

de Caussade, Jean-Pierre. *Abandonment to Divine Providence*. Garden City, NY: Doubleday, 1975.

de Mello, Anthony, S.J. *Sadhana: A Way to God*. St. Louis, MO: The Institute of Jesuit Sources, 1978.

Documents of Vatican II, Walter M. Abbott, S.J., General Editor. New York, NY: Guild Press, 1966.

Dyckman, Katherine Marie, S.N.J.M., and L. Patrick Carroll, S.J. *Solitude to Sacrament*. Collegeville, MN: The Liturgical Press, 1982.

Ensley, Eddie. *Feeling and Healing Your Emotions*. Columbus, GA: Contemplative Books, 1986.

Finley, Mitch. "Recovering the Rosary." *America*. May 7, 1983.

Fischer, Ed. "The Recorded Life." *Notre Dame Magazine*. December, 1981.

Gawle, Barbara. *How to Pray*. Englewood Cliffs, NJ: Prentice-Hall, Inc., 1984.

Grace, John Patrick. *Hearing His Voice*. Notre Dame, IN: Ave Maria Press.

Greeley, Andrew. *The Bottom-line Catechism for Contemporary Catholics*. Chicago, IL: The Thomas More Press, 1982.

Green, Thomas H. *Opening to God*. Notre Dame, IN: Ave Maria Press, 1977.

———. *Weeds Among the Wheat*. Notre Dame, IN: Ave Maria Press, 1984.

———. *When the Well Runs Dry*. Notre Dame, IN: Ave Maria Press, 1979.

Guigo II. *The Ladder of Monks and Twelve Meditations*. Translated by Edmund Colledge and James Walsh. Kalamazoo, MI: Cistercian Publishing Company, 1981.

Hauser, Richard, S.J. *In His Spirit: A Guide to Today's Spirituality*. Mahwah, NJ: Paulist Press, 1982.

———. *Moving in the Spirit*. Mahwah, NJ: Paulist Press, 1986.

Hofinger, Johannes, S.J. *Pastoral Life in the Power of the Spirit*. New York, NY: Alba House, 1982.

Hughes, Gerard. *God of Surprises*. Mahwah, NJ: Paulist Press, 1986.

John of the Cross, Saint. *The Collected Works of Saint John of the Cross*. Translated by Kieran Kavanaugh, O.C.D., and Otilio Rodriguez. Washington, DC: I.C.S. Publications, 1979.

Kelsey, Morton T. *The Adventure Inward*. Minneapolis, MN: Augsburg Publishing House.

———. *The Other Side of Silence*. Mahwah, NJ: Paulist Press, 1976.

Link, Mark, S.J. *Challenge*. Valencia, CA: Tabor Publishing, 1987.

Linn, Matthew, S.J., Dennis Linn, S.J., and Sheila Fabricant. *Prayer Course in Healing Life's Hurts*. Mahwah, NJ: Paulist Press, 1983.

McManus, Jim, C.SS.R. *The Healing Power of the Sacraments*. Notre Dame, IN: Ave Maria Press, 1984.

McNamara, William, O.C.D. *The Human Adventure*. Warwick, NY: Amity House, 1988.

Metz, Barbara, S.N.D. de N., and John Burchill, O.P. *The Enneagram and Prayer*. Denville, NJ: Dimension Books, 1987.

Muto, Susan A. *A Practical Guide to Spiritual Reading*. Denville, NJ: Dimension Books, 1976.

_____. *Pathways of Spiritual Living*. Petersham, MA: St. Bede's Publications, 1988.

Nouwen, Henri J. M. *A Cry for Mercy: Prayers from the Genesee*. Garden City, NY: Image Books, A Division of Doubleday, 1983.

Pearse, Pádraic. *Plays, Stories, Poems*. Dublin: Helican Press, 1980.

Pennington, Basil, O.C.S.O. *Centering Prayer: Renewing an Ancient Christian Prayer Form*. Garden City, NY: Doubleday, 1982.

_____. *Finding Grace at the Center*. Edited by Thomas Keating. Petersham, MA: St. Bede's Publications, 1979.

_____. *Ways of Prayer*. Wilmington, DE: Michael Glazier, Inc., 1982.

Pennock, Michael F. *The Ways of Prayer: An Introduction*. Notre Dame, IN: Ave Maria Press, 1987.

Pilkington, Evan. *Learning to Pray*. London: Darton, Longman & Todd, Ltd., 1986.

Pollard, Miriam, O.C.S.O. *The Laughter of God: At Ease with Prayer*. Wilmington, DE: Michael Glazier, Inc., 1986.

Powell, John, S.J. *The Christian Vision: The Truth That Sets Us Free*. Valencia, CA: Tabor Publications, 1984.

Rosage, David E. *Discovering Pathways to Prayer*. Locust Valley, NY: Living Flame Press, 1975.

_____. *The Sacramental Path to Peace*. Locust Valley, NY: Living Flame Press, 1984.

Shannon, William. *Seeking the Face of God*. New York, NY: Crossroads Publishing Company, 1988.

Shea, John. Article in *U.S. Catholic*. March, 1979.

Tobin, Eamon. *How to Forgive Yourself and Others: Steps to Reconciliation*. Liguori, MO: Liguori Publications, 1983.

———. *Help for Making Difficult Decisions*. Liguori, MO: Liguori Publications, 1987.

———. *The Sacrament of Penance: Its Past and Its Meaning for Today*. Liguori, MO: Liguori Publications, 1983.

United States Catholic Conference. *Behold Your Mother: Woman of Faith*. Washington, DC: United States Catholic Conference, 1973.

———. *Spiritual Renewal of the American Priesthood*. Washington, DC: United States Catholic Conference, 1973.

van Breemen, Peter G. *Certain as the Dawn*. Denville, NJ: Dimension Books, 1980.

van Kaam, Adrian, C.S.Sp. *On Being Yourself: Reflections on Spirituality and Originality*. Denville, NJ: Dimension Books, 1972.

Whalen, William. "How Catholic Prayer Became a Mass Movement." *U.S. Catholic*. September, 1983.

Wolff, Pierre. *May I Hate God?* Mahwah, NJ: Paulist Press, 1979.

Wright, John, S.J. *A Theology of Christian Prayer*. New York, NY: Pueblo Publishing Company, 1979.

To order any book listed in the bibliography, contact your local bookstore.

For information on books published by Liguori Publications, please request a catalog by writing to:

Liguori Publications
Box 060
Liguori, MO 63057-9999